LEAN OUT

A PROFESSIONAL WOMAN'S GUIDE TO FINDING AUTHENTIC WORK-LIFE BALANCE

DAWN L. BAKER, MD, MS

Internet addresses given in this book were accurate at the time it went to press.

This book is intended as a reference volume only, not as a medical manual. The information given here is designed to inspire and inform. It is not intended as a substitute for any treatment that may have been prescribed by your doctor. If you suspect that you have a medical problem, we urge you to seek competent medical help.

Printed in the United States of America

Published in Hellertown, PA

Cover design by Christina Gaugler

Library of Congress Control Number 2023900384

ISBN 978-1-958711-31-6

For more information or to place bulk orders, contact the author or the publisher at Jennifer@BrightCommunications.net.

For my beautiful daughter, Aspen

CONTENTS

PART ONE

"When you stop striving, the consciousness of the Universe awakens inside you and starts to move." —Martha Beck

INTRODUCTION: NOT ON THE LIST

I followed my daughter down the sandy path to our stream. As we walked by, the water glistened in the early morning sunlight. Some parts looked like a big mirror, others like flecks of glitter among the reeds.

She loves the stream so much. She makes up games, jumps across at different points to see how far she can leap, and brings her toys to float them in the water. I love it, too. I love staring at it as I sip my tea. I love taking walks to it. I love how it looks different every time I see it—the water levels and the flow patterns and how it sparkles in the sun differently every day.

Just then, in her muddy frolicking, she said something that made me pause.

"Mom! You jump there, and I'll cross here, and then I'll meet you downstream. Then let's do some stuff that's not on the list!"

"Not on the list?"

"Yeah, like stuff we weren't planning to do. Stuff that's not on the list."

So, that's what we did. We slid down the muddy hill, ate the snow that was still preserved in the shade of the pines, basked in the sun on a huge, smooth log, and cheered the dog as he chased squirrels.

And I appreciated that I've spent a lot of time in my life doing things that are "not on the list."

WHAT LIST?

What list am I talking about? It's the list of how things are supposed to go in the expected trajectory of growing up. It's the list that reads: Study hard in school, get good grades, meet a partner, get a job. Have kids, and keep going on the treadmill. Buy a nicer house and a nicer car and nicer stuff.

I'm talking about the list of things you "should have" accomplished by a certain time. It's the list of ways you should behave when you're a good girl, a respectable woman, a career woman, a responsible mom—the list that tells professional women to "lean in," go for it, and *achieve*.

Here's the thing: The list shames. The list traps. The list destroys. This book is about figuring out what parts of this list should be questioned and maybe even ignored.

WHAT IS #LEANOUT?

Google and Facebook executive Sheryl Sandberg inspired the *Lean In* movement by pointing out the disparity between the opportunities available to women and their positions in the highest leadership roles across numerous industries. She has spoken and written about how women are held back, and how they hold themselves back, from what she sees as their ultimate goals. This book reframes the *Lean In* movement, highlights its potential problems, and shares solutions for how women can navigate professional careers without losing their sanity and health.

Being that I am a physician married to an attorney, many of my examples come from the medical and legal worlds; however, the information in this book could easily be applied to any high-octane career path where work-life balance is an issue. Basically, it applies to anything women are doing these days, be it corporate finance, tech, academia, or even entrepreneurship.

WHAT IS A PROFESSIONAL?

We all work in some capacity. Regardless of trade or field, there is a difference between a worker and a professional. A worker sees a job as a means to an end: a way to make a living and not much more. A professional sees their work as a calling and a journey, one where they can extract fulfillment and grow as a person while they're advancing in their career. This book is for anyone who views themselves as a professional.

Being a professional, however, comes with downsides. Professionals have a level of commitment and integrity that sets them apart but also sets them up for potential stress, burnout, and the trappings of achievement. Over the years, professionalism has even morphed to include a culture of hustle that becomes toxic if it is not questioned.

WHAT IS BALANCE?

The word "balance" conjures up lots of metaphors and imagery—the legal scales, the teeter-totter, the spinning of plates. The term gets a bad rep by many people, especially those who are overworked and overextended. They can't fathom the idea of balance. It's an unachievable construct. "There's no such thing as work-life balance," they'll argue.

I, for one, still love the term—with a few caveats. Balance is best described as a symphony orchestra—where you are the conductor. The different instrument sections represent the multiple roles you play in your life. Some possibilities include parent, child, spouse, friend, doctor, lawyer, accountant, teacher, student, athlete, and artist.

In a classical music composition, sometimes all the instruments are playing together. But the levels of intensity for each are different. They're never playing at the same volume, with the same intensity, at the same time. This would sound grating to the ears. Many people believe balance means equal distribution of all roles and responsibilities at one time, but this is not sustainable nor pleasurable.

At other times, specific instruments have solos. During the solos, other instruments might play very softly in the background, providing supportive tones. Some instruments will be completely silent; this is appropriately called "resting." The players of those instruments are quietly following along with the music, waiting for their turns to contribute.

As such, balance is a symphony of moving parts, of all your varying roles and priorities. While you can "have it all," you can't have it all at once in any sustainable capacity. Things need to move into and out of priority.

WHY WOMEN NEED TO HEAR THIS

All this talk about balance gets to why this book was written for women. On average, women in professional landscapes have an increased number of roles they play—or instruments in their orchestra. Women, whether working or not, shoulder a higher portion of domestic responsibilities than their male counterparts. In a family, there is no denying that a woman bears the physical responsibility of pregnancy, childbirth, and caregiving at the early stages of life. Depending on the number of children a woman has, these increased roles might play a significant part in her life for a number of years.

High-achieving women need to pay attention to their work-life balance now, before they suffer too many costs of the hustle culture. One woman's path to finding it will be different than another's. Balance is highly individual. One person's snappy string quartet piece is another person's full-blown cacophony of sounds, replete with crashing cymbals. This book will give you ideas for how to find the unique, authentic work-life balance that works for *you*.

What you *won't* find here is a commentary on gender bias in the workplace, nor any sort of argument for or against the occupation of certain roles by women, whether at work or at home. Furthermore, this book is not about the currently popular subject of boundaries; at least, it's not overtly about boundaries. The ideas you will read are more about developing self-awareness, which is a cornerstone of the ability to intuitively establish boundaries. You will also experience inspiration from the stories of real women—some referred to by their real first names and others by pseudonyms (noted with a *)—who are courageously designing their own work-life balance now.

CHAPTER 1
A TALE OF TWO WOMEN

"Be aware of the false economy of trying to power through." — Greg McKeown

Dr. A has her highly skilled hands in everything, and she loves it. A well-known physician in a niche area of surgery, she was just named vice chair of her department's research program. She already publishes cutting-edge papers and gives talks all over the world, mentors multiple budding female leaders in the medical school and residency program, and always remembers to drop knowledge bombs and musings on Twitter several times a day.

She and her husband, a psychologist and author, travel on different speaking circuits. They don't mind; they seem to get along better with some intermittent geographical distance. Their daughter attends the private elementary school feeder for the local Ivy League prep school, though their six-year-old son struggles with a learning disability. Each child has a tutor, a music coach, and weekend sports practices. The family relies on two nannies—one for regular business hours and another who works evenings and weekends or stays overnight as necessary.

Busyness is Dr. A's way of life; she feels more comfortable when enveloped in chaos. Thus, she wouldn't think to say no to a new opportunity. Why sell herself short when her career is thriving? Stillness is something she sees as a project for later. Much later.

Dr. A might feel like she's achieved success, fulfillment, and even balance. She's solved many time deficits by outsourcing; the multiple nannies, plus housekeepers and a meal service, are a part of her "village." But is she moving through her days intentionally? Is she in tune with what really matters most to her? Eventually, life circumstances change. Systems and relationships break down. Sometimes, they do so in an instant.

Dr. B was always looking for something different. While surfing the cubicles of tech companies as an engineer, she had visions of the freedom a medical degree would afford her: to live and practice anywhere she wanted (as long as she chose the right specialty). She attended medical school and pursued a career in anesthesiology, which allowed her to travel and rock climb (a significant passion of hers) without an ongoing patient roster looming over her head. She loved learning so many new things in medical school, and the autonomy of internship was so intoxicating that she worked hard enough to receive the intern of the year award. The leaders of her residency program pegged her to be the next chief resident.

On the way to fulfilling Dr. B's original dream, she got side-tracked. Her extensive engineering background helped her quickly and easily understand the ultrasound images and physics of perioperative echocardiography, a very specialized sub-field of anesthesiology. Her supervisors praised her innate skill, and this tempted her to do more. She designed a research project around the subject, presented it at multiple conferences, and pushed to certify her skills by signing up for the national perioperative echocardiography board exam, even before graduation.

At the same time, her performance in other areas of work started to suffer. She found herself depressed and unable to get out of bed without at least a few cups of coffee. Her general lack of energy and interest overshadowed her passions outside of medicine: travel, rock climbing, fitness, and spending time with the love of her life. She and her husband were also having trouble conceiving, causing even more strain on their relationship.

She learned of the term "burnout" and thought, *Maybe this is me*. She saw a doctor and was started on one SSRI ... then two. She continued to struggle while performing procedures and was ridiculed by some of her faculty. But she kept her head down and swallowed her tears, trying to do everything. She still forced herself to get up before 5:00 AM to do workouts prior to her OR shifts, and she continued to go through the motions with rock climbing despite significant fatigue. She made every attempt to show a happy face at work, all the while hiding the shame of knowing she was suffering, and she continued her echocardiography research in her "spare time."

Dr. B's energy levels worsened to the point where any sort of exercise became a chore that required a 30-minute nap afterward. She underwent blood tests and studies, but there was no clearcut answer to what was happening besides depression and burnout. Her doctors had at least figured out the source of her infertility: hypothalamic amenorrhea with resultant ovarian failure. "It was all stress-induced," they said.

Months after the diagnostic odyssey began, Dr. B was forced by a very persistent reproductive endocrinologist to step into an MRI scanner on Easter Sunday. There it was, white as truth on the black screen: a prominent tumor sitting in the middle of her brain. It was the size of an arcade gumball, but it had sprouted tentacles that wrapped around her optic chiasm. A subsequent vision test showed profound peripheral vision loss.

And now it all made sense.

I am Dr. B.

A week after my diagnosis, I was on the table undergoing brain surgery with the head neurosurgeon at the hospital where I trained. One of my faculty professors served as my anesthesiologist. I barely remember wheeling away from the preoperative holding area on a gurney in a midazolam-induced haze, with a hallway of familiar faces turning to look as I was rolled to the operating room. The next thing I knew, I was a patient in the Neuro ICU, lying next to patients I had just recently taken care of.

Everything was now clear: I had fallen completely out of balance to the point of not even knowing that I was seriously ill. I was blind to myself—literally and figuratively, while trying to be everything to everyone. I was too busy to get an MRI. My internal orchestra continued to play a blazingly loud, dizzying number with cymbals crashing … and then it abruptly fell flat to silence. It was like one of those modern, commissioned symphonies—the ones that seem really cool at first but become increasingly uncomfortable to listen to.

After sufficient recovery, I was inspired to closely examine the path I had taken to get there. I was forced into stillness and convalescence, but during that time, I regained the original vision of what I had wanted to do with my life, both inside and outside my profession. More than a decade later, I'm living my authentic balance. If none of this had ever happened to me, where would I be now?

A REFRAME

Let's try this again: Dr. B is a mother and a part-time anesthe-siologist who loves taking care of patients undergoing general, "bread and butter" surgeries. She declined a fellow-ship and cancelled her echocardiography boards in favor of gaining broad-based clinical experience, and more impor-tantly, moving on with her unique vision for her life. Knowing what matters most to them, she and her husband lived simply so they could afford *in vitro* fertilization (a neces-sity for building their family because of the removal of her entire pituitary gland). After years of fertility treatments, they were blessed with a daughter.

Aligned with her original dream of freedom, she now controls her own schedule by taking care of patients as a *locum tenens* (as-needed, daily, or fill-in coverage) physician. Her other work—writing, public speaking, and coaching on wellness and work-life balance—gives her great fulfillment, as does spending lots of time with her family. They recently moved to a large, off-grid homestead in the mountains, where they enjoy the simple pleasures of nature and a slow-paced lifestyle.

A DICHOTOMY

There are many ways women professionals can design their lives to include meaningful work, family, personal growth, and any other endeavors. Both Dr. A and today's Dr. B repre-sent two ends of a broad spectrum. However, they both started their journeys with one thing in common: an intense need to achieve.

Where does this come from? Why is it plaguing women professionals to the point of physical and mental ailments?

And despite far-reaching ramifications that we will discuss in this book, why is it so celebrated by our modern culture?

There are entire Facebook groups, retreats, and conferences dedicated to women like Dr. A who, inevitably, end up crowdsourcing or seeking assistance in figuring out how to improve their work-life balance. What is normally offered or suggested are ways to further outsource: au pairs, meal prep services, virtual assistants, and mother's helpers. While these resources can be helpful, they will not fix a fundamental mismatch of roles and responsibilities to values and desires.

So, many women are prodding along, staying afloat in the chaos. Then, when one little factor changes, all of a sudden, the melody played by their orchestra takes a dissonant turn. You don't have to suffer a major crisis like I did to realize that you are living your life around achievement instead of designing your life the way you want it to be.

Which one of these women are you most like? Which one's life is more appealing to you? Or does the life you envision for yourself look completely different?

EXERCISE: TAKE A GOOD LOOK

Get out a piece of paper and write an assessment of your overall health. How are you *really* doing? What's going well? What would you like to have more of in your life? Some categories to list for your assessment include:

- Physical and mental health
- Spiritual connection
- Relationships
- Personal growth
- Finances

Notice there's no category for "work accomplishments." Where does work fit within the categories I've given you? For example, maybe your work improves your finances but detracts from your mental health. Or maybe your work provides personal growth but decreases your spiritual time.

CHAPTER 2
LEAN IN CULTURE

"The months and years leading up to having children are not the time to lean back, but the critical time to lean in." —Sheryl Sandberg

When Sheryl Sandberg gave her famous graduation speech at Barnard College in 2011, sparking a TEDx talk, a book, and a whole movement, she told graduates to "lean way in"—to forge ahead with ambition and run the world. Those graduates (and many women since) have heeded the call.

Lean In became an entire movement, and women have assumed the mantle. Women now make up almost 60 percent of the undergraduate student population.[1] The number of matriculating women began to eclipse men for law school in 2016[2] and medical school in 2019.[3] Entire professions, such as psychology and veterinary medicine, are predominantly female. The number of chief executives leading Fortune 500 companies has expanded from 7 to 74 in the past 20 years.[4] In this country, we can now say we've had a female Secretary of State, multiple female Supreme Court justices, and even a female Vice President.

RISE OF THE BADASS BOSS BITCH

These trends continue with the next generation of women leaders and professionals on deck. As Sandberg recounted in her book *Lean In: Woman, Work, and the Will to Lead*, one of the graduates who crossed the stage after her speech told her she was the "baddest bitch."[5] These kinds of comments, which might have given a woman pause as recently as the 20th century, are now considered compliments.

Women have assimilated into the well-trodden hustle culture of the corporate workplace and the professional pathways of medicine, law, finance, and tech. In this world, falling behind and asking for help are signs of weakness, and you wouldn't dare miss a day of work due to sickness or a family problem. Showing up despite life's chaos has long been considered a virtue; now, so is the woman trying to do everything at work and at home.

In many dual-income families, women still work a "second shift" comprised of domestic duties and childcare. Slay all day. We can do anything #likeaboss. Side gig? Fitness competition? All while working 50+ hours a week and raising a family? No sweat.

Never has there been a time in our society where women have more opportunities and choices. But are women happier, healthier, and more fulfilled as a result? Let's look at some other parallel trends.

PHYSICAL COSTS

In today's modern, digital society, the health of adult men and women alike is declining. While life expectancy continues to increase by a small amount each year, 15 percent of the US adult population currently has diabetes, and 38 percent of adults meet criteria for prediabetes.[6] CDC NHANES data demonstrate a steady decline in the number of adults who are at a healthy weight, and obesity rates for women are eclipsing those of men.[7] According to the American Heart Association, only one in four people reported spending enough time doing aerobic and muscle strengthening activities to meet current movement guidelines.[8]

Some serious health problems are known to be related to stress and/or long working hours. Numerous studies correlate stress to illnesses, such as viral infections, cardiovascular disease, ulcers, depression, metabolic disturbance, and chronic back pain. In addition, a meta-analysis performed by the World Health Organization found that consistently working more than 55 hours per week was associated with a higher incidence of stroke.[9]

A chronic state of activation in the sympathetic nervous system might be behind many of these physical aberrations. While primitive humans would properly "close" their stress response cycles with rest, family time, or fun, modern humans tend to move from stressful event to stressful event. With the advent of the internet, smart phones, video calls, and the like, there is never a moment in the day when we are forced to have downtime. For many women, the "always on" world is amplified by their additional responsibilities at home; they are on call 24/7.

The *Lean In* movement imagines a world where better work-life policies are commonplace, and all members of organizations flourish under the leadership of women. Yet the professional world is instead reeling from an insidious creep of work time, plus accompanying dysfunction and dissatisfaction. If women leaders are the nurturers, who will play the nurturing role when the leaders themselves are suffering?

PSYCHOLOGICAL COSTS

Burnout—a triad of emotional exhaustion, depersonalization, and diminished personal efficacy—has become an increasingly recognized problem in many workplaces and professions. Deloitte's Workplace Burnout Survey of 2015 reported that a whopping 77 percent of respondents have experienced burnout in their jobs.[10] While 87 percent of respondents reported passion for their work, 64 percent of them said they experience persistent stress on a regular basis. A Bloomberg Law analysis in 2021 revealed that nearly half of attorneys surveyed had experienced burnout in the past year. Almost the same number of respondents reported a decline in their wellbeing, and nearly one third of them experienced new or worsening health issues.[11]

In the physician space, you can't go anywhere without hearing about the pervasive destruction caused by burnout. The Medscape National Physician Burnout, Depression, and Suicide Report surveys more than 15,000 physicians yearly. The reported incidence of burnout is consistently between 40 and 50 percent.[12] Burnout is widely recognized as a source of absenteeism, lost productivity, declining quality of patient care, and even subsequent mental and physical disease.

The top causes of burnout among physicians are long hours, overwhelming workload, and lack of support; these have not changed over the years. For women, burnout and depression go hand in hand. Over the past several years, the Medscape report has listed consistently higher burnout rates for female vs. male physicians. Between 2021 and 2022, four separate surveys found that women physicians are experiencing more burnout than their male counterparts, with specific stressors identified as childcare and household responsibilities.[13]

HAVING IT ALL

While achievement and the outward perception of success have long been virtues in our society, these signals are now even more amplified in the current era of social media connection. Busyness is a badge of honor, one ever-present in our curated social media feeds and filtered photographs. For women, the urge—nay, the duty—to appear perfect is ever-present. It's never been easier to compare all aspects of our lives to others.

These factors—a low threshold to compare, high workloads, diminished work-life balance, and the continuum of burnout —can lead to serious mental despair. While the incidence varies by report, women physicians have a much higher likelihood to die by suicide than female nonphysician counterparts. Attorneys are also experiencing an epidemic of depression, suicide, and substance abuse. The oft-cited "mental load" deepens the costs of this culture for women. It might now be possible to "have it all," but what are the consequences? Having it all does not necessarily translate to the parts of our lives that matter most to us.

EXERCISE: IDENTIFY YOUR SKILLS AND STRENGTHS

Write a list of your skills and strengths. This is not the time to be humble; brag away about yourself through this list. Think about specifics that make you unique; your skill list should include more detail than medicine, law, tech, or accounting. I'm talking about things like cultivating close relationships with clients, communicating complicated concepts to people of all knowledge levels, teaching/mentoring trainees, writing, or speaking.

To get some inspiration, take a look at the lists included in the Resources section. Ask others what they perceive as your greatest skills and strengths. Recall awards you were given during your training and the things supervisors or preceptors wrote about you in evaluations.

LEANNE'S JOURNEY

"There's a stigma even in the concept of leaning out."

When we first met, Leanne* was quick to point out that, though she uses her legal background in her work, she doesn't really practice law. In fact, she practiced law in the traditional sense for a total of 365 days.

"If I had been left to my own devices, I would have gotten a PhD in social psychology," she said. But her parents dissuaded her from academia, wanting to see her pursue a career path with more financial certainty. She also ranked first in her class at her college, so she said, "There was an excitement in the air about my potential." With these urgings, she decided to go to law school.

Leanne became consumed by the admission process—her first red flag. "The legal profession loves to have these institutions that exclude people. There's all these people and institutions in charge of who can access law schools, so once you commit, it's like, 'Oh God, now I've gotta do this!' You're neck deep just to take the test."

By the time Leanne began her law classes, she was already exhausted. She also quickly felt out of place with her classmates. "There's a lot of fluff and self-importance," she said.

Graduation came during the economic crash of 2008, so Leanne took one of few jobs available in finance law. She said that during her time there, "really egregious things happened to me as a woman and as a young associate."

"My first and only year of practicing law was absurd. I was in the law office until 3 in the morning, waiting for some miserable associate from another office to call me, in the middle of whatever hell she was navigating, to give me an assignment. The assignment was like, 'The client doesn't like curly commas, but the documents all have curly commas. They want the font to be the curly comma font, but they don't want curly commas. So, can you go through and change all the commas?' This is real life shit. This is actually a thing I did at 3 in the morning."

Meanwhile, Leanne's husband was doing amazing work for a nonprofit organization. She looked around at the partners in her firm, thinking of all they've sacrificed, and decided she needed to craft an exit.

"I don't need to live this miserable life," she said. "I would rather be happy, as long as I can still have a family, provide for them, and have the fundamentals of life, with some joy release valves (like buying my kids Christmas gifts or going on vacation)."

Keeping her fresh student loan debt in mind, Leanne set out to find a new job outside law. She took an opportunity as a consultant for a startup—despite a $100,000 pay cut. She helped her husband build his nonprofit into a well-known organization. Eventually, she landed a consulting job at the large philanthropic organization she's worked with for the past several years.

Leanne describes herself as an "operative" who gets deployed for certain projects and negotiations. She is a planner, a builder, and a fixer. She loves her work and feels tremendously valued by her organization. "A good legal background allows you to have a mind that can pivot into lots of different places. Your skillset can be applied to anything and everything," she said.

Recently, Leanne, her husband, and their two small children moved from the big city to the country. She negotiated to continue working remotely with her organization. She took another pay cut in the process, but she also started an additional, part-time consulting job for a friend.

"I'm making more money now than I was before, but I've leaned out!" she said. "If I was leaning in, I'd be trying to be the next COO. I'd be in that office [and commuting to the city] ever day busting my ass, but I'm not. Instead, I'm unavailable at noon because that's kid pickup time."

Leanne has come a long way since her days as a miserable associate. She has fused her passion for justice and social causes with logic and problem-solving skills from her legal education. Regarding her current work-life balance, she said, "We've really hit the right notes."

CHAPTER 3
THE COST NO ONE TALKS ABOUT

"The time to scale back is when a break is needed or when a child arrives — not before, and certainly not years in advance." — Sheryl Sandberg

It might be a case of if, not when a child arrives. Professional women are heeding Sandberg's advice to lean in, and it's costing their fertility. This encouragement to keep pushing harder now and worry later assumes that you can start a family at any time along the way. However, the reality of modern family building tells a different story. You might not see a family in the vision you have for your life, but if you do presently or if there is any chance you might in the future, you need to be aware of this hidden cost.

Married at age 25 to a fellow rock climber, I spent the latter half of my twenties and the first half of my thirties living a life of adventure. We traveled by camper truck, RV, and plane with backpacks in tow to climbing locales across the world. Medical school became part of that adventure, and we planned climbing projects and trips around my school schedule. I looked, felt, and performed great, so I assumed I'd have no problem getting pregnant whenever I wanted. I figured that motherhood could wait until after residency. Little did I know, female fertility does not work that way.

Infertility is on the rise in this country, and high-achieving women professionals are suffering most. At present, approximately 13 percent of US couples have infertility.[1] Astonishingly, this rate doubles for couples that include a woman physician.[2] There is no published research to date on infertility among female attorneys, but according to *The American Lawyer,* the issue is becoming increasingly recognized as a problem in the law profession.[3]

Aman is an attorney who, at the same time as announcing her pregnancy on social media, took a leap of vulnerability and disclosed her struggles to conceive. "After more than 1.5 years, blood tests, bodily fluid tests, ultrasounds, and two rounds of fertility treatments … my husband and I are thrilled to share the arrival of our baby," she disclosed. Her post garnered several responses from attorney colleagues who said they too had undergone fertility treatments to have children. One commented, "Almost everyone I know who started to have kids after 30 has had some kind of fertility issue (us included)! When you graduate law school at 25 or older, it makes it hard to have kids earlier than 30."

THE AGE ISSUE

A myriad of factors contribute to infertility, and the exact mechanisms for the current rise in its incidence aren't yet well understood. More than one third of infertility cases also include a male factor as part of the cause.[4] However, one foundational fact stands out among the many explanations: Women are delaying their childbearing years to pursue further education, training, and careers. Compared to women in the 1970s, women today are delaying childbirth by an average of five years. The mean age of an American woman when she becomes a mother is currently 26. However, a women physician on average has her first child at age 31,[5] tacking on another 5 years.

Strong pathophysiological evidence exists to explain a woman's age-related decline in fertility. A woman is born with the absolute number of eggs she will ever have in her lifetime, and as she ages, she continues to lose them through menstruation. In addition, eggs incur DNA damage over time, leading to decreased efficacy. Clinically, this translates to markedly lower pregnancy rates and higher miscarriage rates in women over 30, but especially women over 35.[6] Aging ovaries are less sensitive to the hormones from the brain (or the *in vitro* fertilization medications) that signal ovulation. In addition, there is an age-related increase in incidence of diseases that affect the uterus and ovaries, which, even if resolved, can in turn affect fertility.

The evidence for age-related fertility impairment is so strong that the American Society for Reproductive Medicine and other groups now recommend early evaluation at the slightest hint of trouble conceiving if you're over the age of 35. Instead of having unprotected sex for one year before seeking help (the typical recommendation), reproductive specialists now tell older women to seek evaluation no later than six months after concerted trying.

There's no doubt that the effects of stress can also impair ovulation and other functions needed to achieve and maintain pregnancy. One study found that the miscarriage rate among female surgeons is more than double the national average.[7] An often-cited study of physician fertility asked survey respondents how they would have changed their behaviors had they known fertility would be a problem for them. More than half the women surveyed said they would have attempted to build families earlier. However, doing this in today's *Lean In* culture requires courage to go against the norm.

A PERFECT STORM

If a woman goes straight to medical school from her under-graduate schooling, she will graduate around age 26. By the time she's finished with residency, she'll be at least 30. After that, she's working to hone her newly acquired clinical skills, complete her board certification, and establish herself as a team player in her practice. Likewise, a woman who goes straight to law school will graduate around age 25. She will then sit for the bar and start working as an associate at a law firm. By the time she makes partner, she'll be in her early thirties.

This timing presents a huge problem for women who want to have careers *and* families. The prime years to build your family coincide with the prime years to build your career. Throw infertility treatments into the mix, and you have a perfect storm of stressors that are likely to affect your fertility in a negative way.

The age-related fertility issues discussed above typically begin to manifest in a woman's 30s, but they magnify expo-nentially after age 35. Unfortunately, many healthy high achievers assume they have until this time before they need to worry much about family building. I was one of these women. With an athletic build and a healthy weight, I assumed I had until my late 30s to really get moving on moth-erhood. I also didn't start medical school until I was 28.

When I turned 35 halfway through my residency, my husband and I decided we needed to get serious about having children. At the same time, I couldn't bear the thought of adding anything to my plate, even if it was just a thing in the planning stages. I was already trying to be everything to everyone. My fatigue (later explained by an endocrine tumor) was setting in, my burnout was raging, and every day felt like a chore. Additionally, I had stopped having my period.

Yes, an innocent fertility workup is what led to my cancer diagnosis. After my brain surgery and recovery, I still wanted to become a mother. On top of having permanent infertility related to my brain tumor, I had age-related fertility impairment. After three years of infertility treatments and one miscarriage, I finally had a child … all while working as a physician.

NAVIGATING INFERTILITY WHILE WORKING

Consider what it's like to undergo a typical cycle of *in vitro* fertilization (IVF). You administer nightly hormone injections to grow your follicles in preparation for an egg retrieval procedure. The process usually takes one to two weeks, but you don't know exactly how fast your follicles will grow. For the first week, monitoring consists of just a single blood draw. But during the second half of your stimulation cycle, you must physically go into the clinic for daily transvaginal ultrasounds.

The final call of when the follicles are mature enough for ovulation trigger and egg retrieval is completely out of your control. Every day you head into the clinic wondering: *Will I be having a surgical procedure 36 hours from now?* Once you get the go-ahead to take the injection that triggers all those eggs to ovulate at once, the clock is ticking. You must undergo your egg retrieval (a surgical procedure with anesthesia) before precious time runs out.

Does this process sound compatible with your typical work schedule, to the point where you could complete an IVF cycle without any help from colleagues or notice to managers? Beyond the uncertainty in timing, things sometimes go wrong. Cycles get canceled. Complications occur. Sure, you could use all your vacation time (if you're allowed to ask on that short of notice). It's no wonder that women undergoing fertility treatments meet clinical criteria for depression and/or anxiety more than half the time.[8]

Ingrid is a 49-year-old physician mom of two young children. She met the love of her life a few years after focusing all her energy on a residency and fellowship in family medicine. Because they were both almost 40 years old, she and her husband went right to work building the family they desired. That family was realized through a long journey of infertility treatments, eventually involving donor eggs. Moving to donor eggs was a difficult decision that required the processing of grief and loss, but on top of this stressor, Ingrid also experienced pushback in her workplace.

In Ingrid's practice group, she had the task of coordinating and delivering monthly continuing education lectures. This involved designing a curriculum, choosing relevant topics, and coaching speakers prior to the monthly events. During one of her IVF cycles, she asked her boss if he would be willing to stand in for her as the coordinator if her cycle fell during the days of the planned lectures. The work had already been done, the dates were set, and the presenters were lined up. All she needed was a standby person, and she had done the same for him in the past. But he vehemently refused.

This frustrating conflict eventually led to a very uncomfortable meeting in the presence of her HR representative. When pressured to disclose more than she was willing about her medical situation, she resigned on the spot.

"If it comes down to having a family or being a 'good doctor,' I'm going to choose the first," she told me. "I could have persisted [in that job], but there was no trust. I needed to drop anything that was in my way and let it go."

In a survey I conducted of more than 150 women physicians with infertility, 68 percent admitted they had trouble scheduling their treatments around their work schedules. 30 percent of respondents had changed jobs like my friend Ingrid or had decreased their workload substantially due to their infertility.[9] This unfortunate loss occurs on top of the tragic losses of infertility, but these women rearranged their priorities out of biological necessity. When the window to have a child closes, it closes. Career opportunities will always be there, hopefully with more flexible opportunities in the future.

An outright abandonment of *Lean In* culture will not magically improve women's fertility. Further, not all women professionals list motherhood as a life goal. Nevertheless, having children is an important choice for many. Infertility affects everyone in the workplace—spouses, coworkers, schedulers, and administrators. Unfortunately, it is both a cause and an effect of the high-stress lives of many women professionals. If the current culture doesn't provide enough flexibility to start our families, we will need to redefine the culture one woman at a time.

EXERCISE: WHAT DO YOU REALLY WANT?

What do you really want in your life? Answer this very specifically by visualizing the details. What does your family look like? How many children, if any, do you have? How many days do you want to work, ideally? What other boundaries do you envision related to protecting your family time?

Examples could be no phone calls after 7 PM, no charting at home, and no emails on weekends.

———

SHILPA'S JOURNEY

"It took stepping into the void before realizing that's what my future was."

Shilpa knew she wanted to be a doctor from an early age. Driven by an intense desire to serve others, she chose the specialty of pediatric oncology. She describes this area of medicine as "intense"; oncologists follow their patients from the clinic to the hospital and the ICU, and they even sometimes treat them in their homes. "It is a serious commitment that is only feasible if you have a strong support network to take care of people in a way that doesn't prevent you from being able to take care of yourself," she said.

Shilpa loved her job in a small private practice, but some family circumstances caused her to question her identity as a physician. Her mother was diagnosed with multiple cancers, which led her family to seek genetic testing. Shilpa found out she inherited a gene from her mother that significantly increases her risk for multiple types of cancer. Thus, she and her husband made the choice to use IVF with genetic screening to build their own family.

"I tried doing IVF while I was in clinical medicine … and it was really challenging," Shilpa said. Working in a small group, she found it very difficult to make sure her patients were getting the care they needed while she was undergoing cycles. "I felt like I wasn't able to give my patients the quality care that I wanted to give and still pursue the IVF path," she said.

She knew she wanted children in her future, and she at least wanted to give the whole IVF process a try. Her second round of IVF had very poor results: no euploid, genetically normal embryos. At the same time, Shilpa had become her mother's primary caregiver after a diagnosis of leukemia—the cancer that ultimately took her life. The stress was overwhelming.

"It wasn't fair to my group, and it wasn't fair to my patients," Shilpa said. The group tried to accommodate her needs, but all the members carried tremendous clinical loads. She also admitted, "sometimes I need to be there for myself and not be available for others." Looking down the long road of using the IVF process to have multiple children, along with the uncertainty of her own future health, "I had to change my work environment so I could do what I wanted to do… in a way that made me feel like I could do it with integrity." She made the difficult decision to leave clinical medicine when she found an alternative job as a remote research physician for a pharmaceutical company.

Shilpa took two months off all work duties and resumed her IVF treatments after starting the new job. Fortunately, her most recent egg retrieval was much more successful. To what extent does she think a shift in her stress levels played a part in this success? "I think it was huge," she said. "While there is evidence [on both sides] … for me, I saw a big difference."

The most difficult part of this whole journey for Shilpa was separating herself from the vision of her career she had held since childhood. "I had to go through that process cognitively and then feel okay about it emotionally," she said. She leaned on her background in spirituality and personal growth to remember that she's not defined by her external circumstances (see Chapter 6 for more on this subject).

In addition to having the ultimate flexibility, Shilpa is loving the work she's doing in her new job. Her research focuses on immunotherapy—an area of cancer treatment where she already had great interest. "I love the work I'm doing right now… I'm able to help people on a much larger scale than I was before," she said. She is honored to do her job and feels it is still in service to her patients. She's now looking forward to getting pregnant with one of her stored embryos.

CHAPTER 4
A CULTURE SHIFT

"A great day is when I rush home from the craziness of the office to have dinner with my family." —Sheryl Sandberg

Yes, this is quoted word for word from the book *Lean In*. Sandberg even describes saying something of the sort in an interview, then backpedaling because of the shame she felt from making the statement. It took her significant internal work to be able to get to the point where she could … wait for it … *leave the office at 5:30.* She qualifies this by admitting that she still goes online to work later in the evening.

It has to be okay to want more than this.

Sadly, the hard-driving work culture of professions such as law and medicine has been around for a long time, and the assimilation starts early. In the name of "professionalism," medical students are taught to detach from emotion when facing patients and colleagues. Falling ill is a sign of weakness; there is no way you would ever "call in sick" unless you're *actually dying*.

Law students learn the cutthroat nature of competition and comparison when they discover pages ripped out of the class community books and secret outline-making in early study groups. These behaviors, which also show up in other professions and work environments, are not only ingrained; they are revered. Further, once the rigors of training are over, the behaviors don't disappear. These portions of the "hidden curriculum" become unwritten rules for our everyday lives.

In order to mitigate the burdens on women that often accompany this culture, there are now entire businesses dedicated to work-life balance solutions: meal prep services that range from boxes of ingredients to a personal chef, au pair referral networks, and Facebook groups with thousands of members "empowering" women professionals to make more money, start side businesses, and crowdsource their work-life balance. While I'm not against using any of these resources, what I'm talking about goes beyond merely outsourcing your to-do list.

Sometimes the best solution is to remove things from your life as opposed to adding more.

THE RULES

We each live our lives by unwritten rules. Some are easy to identify, especially when it comes to expectations at work. Notable examples include:

"A good doctor puts patients first."

"If I want to make partner, I have to go above and beyond the required billable hours."

"I can't be the last one in the office in the morning or the first one out the door in the evening."

At the same time, we each have unwritten rules that govern the judgements we make on ourselves and others. These could be steeped in our cultural backgrounds, upbringing, and life experiences. They might be thoughts like:

"In order to be loved, I must …"

"Because I am a victim, I cannot …"

"In order to be a good _____ (insert doctor, lawyer, wife, parent, child, etc.), I must …"

We might not even realize these rules exist in our brains. If you reflect on your actions just over the past day or two, you'll likely find some of these hiding in the crevices. Unwritten rules govern our behavior, and sometimes that's just fine. The key is in deciding if they're *really true.* Are you living by rules that don't align with your values or vision for your life?

When we fall into a culture that doesn't quite feel right, it can affect our health. Shame and authenticity expert Brené Brown, PhD, said, "The space between your professed values and your practiced values is where burnout lives." Inauthenticity is an energy drain that is linked to stress, anxiety, and depression.[1]

Where does the line fall between professionalism and authenticity? If you want to lead a more balanced life as a professional, this is something you're going to have to figure out for yourself. No one else is going to solve it for you. Yes, the system is broken. Professionals are experiencing moral injury. And unfortunately, systems and cultures don't change quickly.

You can wait around for yours to evolve. You can even try to change the system … or you can take your health and happiness into your own hands.

It doesn't matter how small of a shift against the culture you want to make; to become the truest sense of yourself in this world, you must identify, question, and unlearn the offending rules your brain has accepted as truth. Author Elizabeth Gilbert, speaking on what life coach Martha Beck has taught her, said, "Your intuitive nature will take care of everything. In order to listen to it, you have to step away from trauma, and you have to step away from culture."

A WAKEUP CALL

Facing a frightening diagnosis, surgery, and lifelong medical treatment, I stared my own mortality in the eyes. It brought everything, including my "rules," into immediate examination. Suddenly, I had nothing to lose. I gave up the idea of pursuing the fellowship or the echocardiography boards. It wasn't because I was afraid that I couldn't do them. I gave them up because I realized they were antithetical to the life I really wanted.

When I was sick but didn't know why, struggling with the motivation to even go to work each day, I longingly thought back to my time as an engineer. Why had I gone to medical school when I could have just continued to help make faster computer chips? On the darkest of days, I even wondered why I hadn't taken the path of becoming a barista. I mean, I do love coffee. But once I was diagnosed with a brain tumor and optic nerve compromise, and I laid there on that cold, hard operating table wearing only a patient gown like all the patients I had treated in their most vulnerable states, I remembered.

In my convalescence, I realized what was most important to me. I had just experienced a major health event, but it could have been so much worse. Through caring for patients, I had experienced plenty of sad … and this wasn't it. I still mostly "had my health," and I had serious hope that I could gain back my vitality and joy for living.

I remembered why I had gone into medicine in the first place —to afford a unique kind of freedom that wasn't available to me in the niche industries that make up chemical engineering careers. As a doctor, I could live and work anywhere I wanted because all humans need medical help (not just those in San Jose or Houston or Phoenix). I could also interact with a wide variety of people, from patients to families to other healthcare team members.

So then, *why* had I been on this path that would peg me into a very specialized niche in my chosen medical specialty? One where I would have to live in a large city and work for either a huge group or an academic institution? One that would narrow the types of patients I served as opposed to the diversity of experience I craved?

THE HEDONIC TREADMILL OF ACHIEVEMENT

In the third grade, my teacher identified me as a high achiever. Aside from recognition, he "rewarded" me with the opportunity to write an extra report on a topic of my choosing every month. Being young and not having many commitments on my time, I happily accepted the additional challenge and added work. This began the formation of some of my unwritten rules about what is required for success—and what is required for praise.

Achievements fulfill the higher need that many humans have for accomplishment. We want to meet challenges and make contributions. We want to belong in our cultures. Achievement, however, is a quest that's never-ending. It can be addictive—even dangerous.

Hedonic adaptation is the concept where, despite the occurrence of significant positive or negative events, your set point for happiness tends to return to a baseline over time.[2] Despite experiencing a joyful moment, such as a marriage, a job promotion, or even winning the lottery, our happiness levels eventually go back to where they were before the external input that incited the perceived change. The classic example of how this works is when you buy a new car. At first, you admire your car and notice its pristine beauty or increased performance over your old car with every drive. Over time, the shiny newness fades, and driving the car doesn't give you that same novel joy that it once did. It's just an okay car.

Then, you feel the longing to get another car. That's where the treadmill part comes in. Our expectations rise to meet the new status quo, which prompts us to seek out more ways to increase our perceived level of happiness. So, how does this apply to achievement? You likely grew up being told you're smart. You might have been particularly good at math or English or something else. Getting praise gave you a sense of happiness, acceptance, importance, and maybe even love.

You continue to do more of what you're "good at." As you mature, you choose to focus your efforts on areas of self-perceived strength. You keep achieving, so people praise you more … and they reward you with more responsibilities.

Former lawyer turned writer and happiness expert Gretchen Rubin said, "Making partner at a law firm is like winning a pie eating contest and being told that the prize is more pie." This pattern continues from your school days straight into your career. Achievement is met with more praise and an accompanying wider set of responsibilities, because *you do such good work, you can handle it.*

Our self-worth also gets woven into the treads on the treadmill of achievement. We form more unwritten rules related to our performance:

"I cannot fail, or people won't love me."

"I should be grateful I was given this opportunity/job/spot in a class."

"What I really want to do with my life isn't possible because it's not reimbursable/billable/valuable."

Soon, our lives are filled with tasks, goals, and projects that, despite feeding our sense of self-worth, relevance, or importance, may or may not be related to what *actually matters* to us. Priorities and time spent begin to misalign. Values and actions diverge. Roles and interests become mismatched … all while we're not really looking.

EXERCISE: HOW ENTRENCHED ARE YOU ON THE TREADMILL OF ACHIEVEMENT?

Ponder these questions. Consider writing your thoughts about each as a journal entry. There are no right or wrong answers, nor is there a number of affirmatives that deem you "achievement addicted." Only you will know how you really score.

1. What are your top three priorities right now?

2. Are you spending your time on your top three priorities, or on something else?

3. Who are your role models, and why?

4. Could you see yourself doing anything different than your profession?

5. What would you do if you were suddenly disabled and could not perform the tasks required of your profession?

6. Do you have difficulty relaxing during your down time?

7. Do you feel a scarcity of time—that there's not enough time in the day or days in the week to get things done?

8. Whose opinions matter to you most?

9. How do you feel when you see a colleague or friend experiencing success or receiving praise?

10. If you were told you only had six months to live, what would be the first thing you'd do?

———

BC'S JOURNEY

"You can't really become or do something unless you imagine it in your head."

Over the past decade, BC has gone from feeling like a "widget on an assembly line" to living an "alternative lifestyle professional journey on my terms." She started her medical career as a hospitalist in New York, but when she and her husband (an emergency medicine physician) both became despondent about their jobs, they decided to make a big lifestyle change and moved across the country to Florida.

"Financially, it was the best thing we ever did (leaving the northeast)," she said. "We wanted our kids to be able to run around outside, and they do. They come back covered in mud!"

At a young age, BC knew she wanted to live a life less ordinary. She found an early role model in the German "mother" she had as an exchange student during a gap year in Europe. She witnessed this woman, an ophthalmologist, working part time while raising three children and carving out space in their lives for travel and adventure. When BC and her family moved to Florida, she decided to take a page out of her

European experience and design a life that does not revolve solely around work. First, she pursued a fellowship in the area of internal medicine she loved the most: palliative care. Afterward, she began a part-time position as a palliative care physician in the Veterans Affairs system.

Over the years, BC's work environment slowly grew toxic. "It was a very hostile work environment, and it was department-specific," she said. BC decided to retire because the only other alternative workplace in her geographic area would not consider hiring a part-time physician. She and her husband had simplified their lives to reach financial independence, so work became optional.

"We always had the goal of using money to control our time," she said. Little did she know, retirement was not for her. "I went crazy," she said.

Then the pandemic happened. Her state asked for physicians to come out of retirement, so within one year of retiring, BC returned to medicine.

"And I'm so glad I did," she said.

She's now in a per diem position in a great hospital system with supportive coworkers and supervisors. She realized that her desire to retire was driven not by a dislike of medicine, but by a role mismatch.

Aside from her part-time practice of palliative care medicine, BC is also an author. She wrote a book about the Financial Independence Retire Early (FIRE) movement specifically for physicians. She is also working on multiple novels as part of what she calls a "DIY MFA." Her clinical time takes up approximately 50 shifts per year. BC derives joy and purpose from her work, always reminding herself what a privilege it is to serve her community in this capacity.

While she says that the security and freedom of financial independence have been the best things about taking her unconventional path, BC admits that it's tough being different from her peers.

"I feel like parts of me are split," she said.

She doesn't fully fit into the author world, nor does she completely feel comfortable in the physician community. She recounts physician friends visiting her home once and declaring, "You have no furniture! You have no TV!"

BC has dealt with feeling like an outsider by getting coached, going to conferences, and carving out her own slice of community. She's active in a local Women in Medicine group, and she regularly attends conferences and retreats with other physicians on the topics of women's issues and finance. Above all, she credits coaching for her greatest growth. When asked what she would tell her younger self, she said, "Aside from getting therapy sooner, I would get coaching sooner. I wouldn't be where I am today [without it]."

BC's unique career path demonstrates that leaning out does not have to mean retiring from your profession. You can derive joy and meaning from your work while at the same time not becoming consumed by it. The key is being open to making changes to your plans.

"All of adult life is continuously working what works in the moment, and then you pause and shift and pivot to something else," she said.

CHAPTER 5
STEPPING OFF THE TREADMILL

"You do well, and people give you praise, and you want to continue doing well… But I hadn't asked myself the 'why' and really developed a sense of self-worth and self-love independent of those achievements." —Physician and Crossfit champion Julie Foucher[1]

In *Lean In*, Sheryl Sandberg mentions seeing women "leaning back" at the boardroom table, as if to say, "I'm not sure I want to commit at this level," or "I'm not cut out for being at the table." She tells women that the time to pay attention to work-life balance is when something happens or when a child is born. I propose that time is NOW. You do not want to get to a point when, as she says, "a break is needed" because most likely, you'll be suffering with one of the costs mentioned earlier.

It is not lazy, irresponsible, nor unprofessional to consider, and possibly give up, your position on the treadmill of achievement. On the contrary, cultivating self-awareness and making needed changes to your work-life balance is the most responsible thing you can do—for yourself, for your family, and for your patients and clients. It takes courage to step off the familiar treadmill and onto an unworn, unconventional path to your own fulfillment.

This is not about leaning back. It's about leaning out.

Women are particularly susceptible to trappings of the tread-mill of achievement. Women consistently score higher than men on the trait of agreeableness in psychological testing.[2] They often have a difficult time "rocking the boat" and tend to lean toward maintaining cooperation and harmony. As Sheryl Sandberg pointed out in *Lean In*, women are, on aver-age, less confident in their abilities, especially those that confer adaptability and innovation. In her mind, women tend to lean back instead of taking on a big project or speaking up about a promotion, and thus they do not end up on the path to coveted leadership roles.

In my mind, this is not the issue. Yes, women frequently lack the self-confidence to ask for exactly what they want. The problem is, in many cases, they don't even know what they want because they've been keeping their heads down on the treadmill, doing the work, and watching their feet pound the treads, all the while absorbing outside messages about what they think they should want.

TRUTHS OF THE TREADMILL

- Even though it costs a lot to replace you, you are easily replaceable.
- There is no loyalty in the workplace.
- You are not a savior. Your clients and patients will be okay without you.

- Many people are worried about what others think of them, but most of the time people are too busy thinking about themselves.
- You can have allegiance to your clients and patients—and also to yourself at the same time.

WHAT'S KEEPING YOU FROM LEANING OUT

The momentum of the treadmill is so strong, it can feel daunting to think about taking that first step onto solid ground. Why might you not feel so courageous to ask for a unique work schedule, to take an unexpected career turn, or to say no to increased responsibilities? Here are some common thoughts and feelings that might be causing you to refrain from leaning out. By identifying which ones apply to your situation, you will learn to separate the truth from the fiction.

Fixed Mindset

I grew up thinking that all my personality traits were set in stone. I was smart, good at English, and I loved art and music. On the flip side, I was decidedly *not* outdoorsy, rugged, nor strong. Yet somehow, I ended up rock climbing, living on the road, and pursuing scientific career paths. My choices defied so many of the things I had been told in those early adult years—by my parents, my teachers, other people, and even me—about who I was. I ended up accidentally proving the tenets of what psychologist and researcher Carol Dweck refers to as the Growth Mindset.[3] People who have a growth mindset view weaknesses, challenges, and setbacks as opportunities to learn. They realize they can change their circumstances with persistence, new learning, and hard work. People who continue with a fixed mindset do not open themselves to the possibilities outside their comfort zones.

Neuroplasticity research has shown that our brains can rearrange their well-worn circuitry of thinking to form new pathways.[4] We can learn new skills, take new paths, and adapt to change. When you embrace a growth mindset, you release limiting beliefs about what you can and can't do. Suddenly, all the things you've written off about your work or life situation seem possible.

Victim Mindset

As an extension of the fixed mindset, you might see yourself as a victim of your circumstances. This results in a feeling of powerlessness. In the burnout realm, there is a lot of talk about moral injury. The system is broken, and there is evidence of it everywhere. A study of primary care physicians found that to provide adequate preventative and chronic disease care based on payor standards, doctors would need 27 hours per day.[5] High workplace demands with low resources in a toxic culture of favoritism and non-transparency have been described commonly in law firms.[6]

While these problems should not be diminished, there exists a duality. Systems and organizations will need to change, and increased awareness of the costs of this culture is helping. You cannot control the speed at which the change takes place, but you can control your thoughts, feelings, and actions. You don't have to wait for things at work to get better; the change must come from within you.

Doubt

Doubt in your abilities—whether they be work-related skills or other abilities such as negotiation, leadership, or entrepreneurial prowess—might be keeping you from leaning out. These feelings are very common, especially for high achievers. Impostor Syndrome, a condition where self-doubt is amplified to the point of feeling fraudulent, has been reported as high as 70 percent among doctors and lawyers in multiple studies.

Recognize that you are not alone. Famous performers, notably Barbra Streisand, Tom Hanks, and Maya Angelou, expressed feeling like an impostor. The rise of the internet and social media has given us access to more information and resources for skills acquisition than ever before; a regular person could actually learn to perform like the ranks of those mentioned above. The beauty of this is that, as summarized by creative entrepreneur Chase Jarvis, no one cares about your pedigree anymore. "What was considered 'standard' for our parents is no longer a reality," he said.[7]

You have every right to be where you are now, and you can do anything you want with the skills you've acquired. The sky's the limit. Remind yourself of your many amazing accomplishments. Revisit your photo archive, journals, resume, CV, and brag sheets to jog your memory. Reframe the doubts that show up in your head by employing a growth mindset as above. Maybe you haven't mastered that specific skill … *yet*.

Worry

Maybe what you want deep down is something entirely different than what you're doing now. Are you thinking about a job change, a deep cut to your hours, starting your own business, or maybe even a radical shift in your career? You might be worried about things like what your coworkers, friends, or family will think about it.

One of my favorite internet memes says, "Stop worrying about other people liking you. Most people don't even like themselves." Interestingly, research on what is called the Beautiful Mess Effect reveals that when people show vulnerability (in asking for help or other scenarios), they are viewed by others in a more positive light.[8] It's difficult for many of us to accept, but here is one truth:

What other people think does not matter.

And even that is questionable because the other people are likely not even having thoughts about you. The only opinion that matters is your own. Write that down. Say it to yourself over and over again.

Another common worry is about money. *How can I afford to make a big change?* Don't let a lack of planning up until this moment deter you. Think of the associated nonmonetary costs: What if continuing in your current situation causes you health problems, family issues, or a divorce? Being that you're a high achiever, here is another tactic: Start saving money now. Do whatever you can: Open a separate account, cut back on one expense and earmark that unspent cash for your emergency fund, etc. There will never be a perfect time when you feel financially secure enough to make a big switch in your career, but having taken some proactive steps will give you the confidence that you're on the right track.

Brené Brown, PhD, defines worry as the thinking part of anxiety, the negative thoughts about bad things that might happen in the future. As such, you can train your brain to bring yourself back to the present moment and out of the doom-and-gloom future. We'll talk more about simple mindfulness techniques in Chapter 9.

Fear

Evolutionarily, fear is a swift, present-moment emotion that protects us from physical harm. If you feel paralyzed by fear of leaning out, question what you're really most afraid of. Likely, it's not impending harm. What you're probably feeling is anxiety and vulnerability at the idea of exposing your authentic self and your true desires. In *Atlas of the Heart*, Dr. Brown also discusses how anxiety and excitement register similarly in the brain.[9] Perhaps what you're feeling can be reframed in a positive light.

In high-achieving professions with so many tests and hoops that must be jumped through, we've been conditioned to fear failure. Failure doesn't have to be a bad thing; it's an essential part of life! We can reframe failure as well. What if it were easy? What if no one batted an eye?

Coaching client Rebecca* knew from the start that she wanted to negotiate lower work hours for her private practice anesthesiology job, but she felt stuck in her own mind. She was teetering on the edge of burnout. Long days in the operating room and frequent nights on call drained her energy to the point where she wasn't able to be present with her toddler when she was home. There was only one other physician in her group who worked a reduced clinical load, and that person had done a poor job of negotiating and maintaining the necessary boundaries.

Rebecca could not follow in those footsteps; she would have to design and propose her own arrangement to the partners. However, she was relatively new to the practice, only a couple years out of fellowship. She feared what the partners would think of her, and she feared repercussions. Her thoughts were:

It will look bad for me to ask for a lighter schedule at this point in my career.

I'm one of the only specialty fellows; what will they think?

What will I do if I completely screw this job up?

Rebecca was still in the fear-based mindset many of us can relate to: residency mode. She still saw herself as the lowest of the low, paralyzed by the fear that if she messed up, she could be "hurt" (usually with more work and less sleep) by people more senior. Many physicians in training live in this mode for years, and it does not just fade away once the training phase is complete. This thought pattern becomes ingrained, and it's tough to get rid of.

After finally letting go of the fear and asking for what she needed, Rebecca said to me in follow up, "I was surprised there wasn't more blowback." Work became pleasurable again, and she was able to view call nights as a challenge instead of dreading them. Most importantly, she was able to enjoy being with her family again during critical years of her child's life.

There's rarely as much blowback as you think there will be. People are too caught up in their own dramatic stories to care much about what you do.

Guilt

You might have guilt related to leaning out because the change you want to make means you'd have to leave your patients, clients, coworkers, or other team members. Maybe you feel guilty that you're not dedicated enough to the calling of your chosen profession. You "wasted a spot" in medical school, law school, or the like—as the trolls put it.

The feeling of guilt comes from not meeting a set standard or not following a rule. While guilt is a very useful and impor- tant emotion when we've *actually* done something wrong, it muddies the waters when the deviation in question is from a completely made-up standard. You might have made it up, or it might have become fabricated by the culture. Pick a rule that you identified from the previous chapter and remember that rule might not be based on anything other than arbitrary standards you think you need to meet. If you lean out, are you doing something wrong? Who are you hurting? It's not your job to be a savior.

Shame

While guilt stems from feeling you've *done* something wrong, shame encompasses a wider feeling that you *are* what is wrong. Shame burrows deeply into your sense of self-worth. The needs to do more and to be perfect are both rooted in shame. Many women (me included) grew up wanting everyone to like them. We have historically felt the need to prove we're worthy by doing but also prove we're likable by appearing perfect and never "rocking the boat."

The foundation of shame is judgement and lack of love for yourself. So, to stand up for yourself and what you want out of your life, you must bring the love back. Cultivate self-awareness: learn your triggers, the origin of your shame (usually things said and done when you were growing up), and your default coping mechanisms. Grow your self-compassion by treating yourself the way you would treat a dear friend, or better yet, your own child. Depending on how deep your shame runs, it might be a good idea to work with a therapist and/or a coach. (See Chapter 9 for more on these concepts.)

All-or-Nothing Thinking

When I was burned out and ill, I pondered the ultimate question: Should I quit medicine and go work at Starbucks or get a job at the local climbing gear shop? I was blinded by all-or-nothing thinking: If I couldn't practice anesthesiology at the highest, most prestigious level, then I should just forget it and go work retail. What about the in between? If I had really gone down the rabbit hole of leaving my residency, there are so many other things I could have investigated: medical devices, pharma, medical writing, and consulting. As time goes on, this kind of list only grows when you suffer from all-or-nothing thinking.

A complete pivot to a different industry could be the solution to your work-life balance problems. But if you're feeling unbalanced in your current work situation, that doesn't mean you have to leave. Order a different arrangement that's not on the menu: part time, virtual days, job sharing, a sabbatical, or even just a shift in roles. Just because no one has asked for it before doesn't mean you can't be the first. There are so many shades of grey in between the black and white that most people see at work.

Sunk Cost Fallacy

An extension of all-or-nothing thinking is the sunk cost fallacy. It's easy to think that if you spent so long training to work in your field, you have to do it "all the way" in order to be worthy. Any career path will give you specific skills and also cultivate your innate strengths. Do you know what yours are? (Make sure to complete the exercise at the end of Chapter 2.) They can likely translate to many different work possibilities.

Remember that, while you might still owe money in loans related to schooling, you owe no one any particular amount of time. You did not pursue your profession to feel enslaved by it. Everything has a cost, and as discussed above in the *Worry* section, that includes *not* taking action.

Confusion

Maybe things have been feeling "off." Perhaps you're developing some negative habits or even some health issues. Maybe you're overwhelmed by the sheer amount of things on your to-do list on a daily basis. You might feel the need for change, but you don't even really know what you want. In many of my Facebook groups for women physicians, I frequently read anonymous posts that start like these:

"I'm trying to decide if I should leave clinical medicine or if I'll have regrets."

"I'm not sure what I'm looking for: commiseration or permission."

"I really need some advice on a life-changing decision."

Asking for advice from others is fine, but the root of confusion is a fundamental lack of understanding of yourself. Read on for ways to take much-needed time for self-inquiry and develop deeper self-knowledge, which will help you figure out your direction.

The rest of this book focuses on how to find the courage to move forward and design your authentic work-life balance. Courage doesn't have to mean quitting. It means showing the world more of what makes you *you*, being true to what you value most, and being unapologetically determined to take the steps. It means showing yourself the kind of integrity you've worked so hard to bring to your clients, colleagues, and patients.

EXERCISE: BREAK THE RULES

You don't have to experience a major crisis to wake up to a life you didn't really sign on for. You can break your own rules. First, you must identify them. A good way to start is to think of all the roles you have in your life—all the instruments in your orchestra. Some that might come up for you include doctor, lawyer, engineer, dentist, accountant, mother, daughter, sister, wife, caregiver, athlete, entrepreneur, even just "woman." Write them all out on a piece of paper or in a journal, and then brainstorm the unwritten rules you abide by for each role. While reflecting on all the rules you've identified, ask yourself:

Is this rule absolutely true?

Is this rule serving me?

Where did this rule come from?

What would really happen if I break this rule?

MILENA'S JOURNEY

"Do what you love, and the money will follow."

Milena gave this advice for anyone who has concerns about how they might weather the financial insecurities of leaning out. She spent years in marketing for high-powered clients, including a ski resort chain in the Lake Tahoe area. As an early adopter of marketing in the digital age, making herself always available had its costs.

"I ended up working with phenomenal clients all around the world but at the same time sleeping with my phone," she said.

She decided that this kind of work life was not sustainable.

"I wanted to find a way that I could fit my work into my life, instead of the other way around," she said.

She and her husband decided to take a 10-day trip to Baja California Sur, Mexico. Little did they know, there would be absolutely no internet available. The time in solitude, in nature, and away from devices allowed her to be present and reconnect with her values. She also connected with her fears, which put her in a deep state of flow; she was forced to pay complete attention in the moment.

On this trip, they decided to try kiteboarding lessons. "It was a super scary experience, and the only time I was ever able to fully focus on something outside of work." Milena had spent plenty of time outside hiking and skiing before, and she was no stranger to meditation and yoga. But nothing had ever given her that complete sense of flow like kiteboarding. Also, she said, "The feeling of fear made me feel human and vulnerable."

During this experience, Milena realized she had been missing out on living and needed to return to finding joy in things outside of work. That intense flow experience—the sense that time either speeds up or stands still while you are fully engaged and immersed in an activity—also opened up a world of inquiry for Milena; she immersed herself in studies of mindfulness practices and the neuroscience of wellbeing. This is where her business, Unhustle, was born.

Through her company, Milena challenges others to examine their work addiction and build in adequate recovery systems through play, immersive experiences, and mindfulness practices. Her daily work now looks like deep, creative time developing visual messaging, writing projects, corporate wellness offerings such as speaking and retreats, and a book. This is sandwiched by her own mindfulness practice and time spent outdoors, doing things she loves on the water, like kite- and paddleboarding. And Milena and her husband recently moved full-time to Baja.

While Milena now defines success as being grounded in her values, living in a place she loves, and doing what she loves, she is still in the position where she must market herself to spread her message. Accordingly, her biggest challenge is still "dealing with my ego and my internal hustle." She manages her comparison to others by having a strong belief in why she made the changes she did.

After a transformation born out of fear, Milena's best advice for women who find themselves stuck on the treadmill of achievement is to find your courage.

"Be more pirate," she says. "Have a purpose and a mission you're willing to die for, even if it's just your family."

She encourages others to view their worries about financial insecurity by reversing the way they look at money. "Wealth is so much more than money," she says. Wealth is your health, your relationships, and your sense of purpose and contribution. Many people have it backward in that they think making lots of money will facilitate fun, passion, and purpose later in life. Milena urges you to search out your "why" *now*, and the money will follow.

PART TWO

"Whatever you can do, or dream you can, begin it. Boldness has genius, power, and magic in it." —W.H. Murray

CHAPTER 6
HUMAN BEING VS. HUMAN DOING

"It takes courage to grow up and become who we really are." — E.E. Cummings

Figuring out "who you really are" is foundational to leaning out. Living life by your rules instead of defaulting to someone else's work ethic and culture requires a deep understanding of yourself. So, who are you, really?

What do you say when people ask you to describe yourself? Likely, you start off with physical descriptors. Then you might mention your job and maybe some of the other titles you hold, such as wife, mother, friend, etc. When asked how to describe who he really is, author Jason Reynolds said we're each just the person in the shower—the place where we're naked and washed clean of everything[1].

We are who we are when no one else is looking and we're doing nothing.

Just imagine how your true self is revealed when you're doing nothing. All the doing, all the striving, all the accomplishments, titles, and embellishments are removed. Spiritual expert Eckhart Tolle said, "The joy of Being, which is the only true happiness, cannot come to you through any form, possession, achievement, person, or event…. It emanates from the formless dimension within you, from consciousness itself and thus is one with who you are."[2]

We start out this way. As we grow up, we form personality traits and default thought patterns. We also naturally begin to develop a protective armor around our core. This is often referred to as the ego. The ego is basically the part of us that thinks. The ego is not to be confused with "having an ego," such as being arrogant or narcissistic. It is the part of us attached to our physical forms, the roles we play in life, and the things around us. It is the sense of self that is completely identified with our thoughts.

Think back to your earliest years of school. We typically begin to form our longer-term, episodic memories around age four to five. However, it is typically not until age eight or nine that the ego begins to form. When I recall this time of my life, I envision a girl running around in a rainbow-striped swimsuit on a hot California summer day, playing with her little sister on the lawn. The Beach Boys, Chicago, or Crosby, Stills & Nash are blaring over the patio speakers.

Why are these details important? They're not, except to say that the elements of this scene are part of "who I am":

- Outdoors
- Movement
- Play
- Music
- Warm sunny days
- Family

These kinds of elements make up who you are. In contrast, you are not the typical way you likely describe yourself. This is the scaffolding your ego has formed:

- Appearance
- Abilities
- Jobs
- Titles
- Accomplishments
- Possessions

"WHAT DO YOU DO?"

Seeing yourself through your ego lens is one thing. The common question, "What do you do?" goes a step further. It is a deeply rooted signal in *Lean In* culture that assumes *doing* is of paramount importance. Your profession is only one tiny part of you, only one part of what others see from the outside. There is also the entire you on the inside.

We are human beings, not "human doings." We are not defined by our jobs, our achievements, our possessions, nor our titles. Achievements are amazing, satisfying, and something to be celebrated, but we must learn to honor our roles and functions in the world without becoming totally identified with them.

You have an inherently beautiful essence. It's an essence that's still present, even after all these years of triumphs and failures, of choices that led you down very specific paths and made you who you *think* you are today. If someone asks you to talk about yourself, what do you say? What go-to forms automatically come out of your mouth? They're a part of you, but they are *not you*.

All you really have to say when someone asks is, "I am."

THE ART OF DETACHMENT

To truly see yourself and live for yourself alone, you must peel away the scaffolding that has formed around you. Doing this might sound theoretical and daunting. Tolle has also said, "If you cannot look through this collective delusion, you will be condemned to chasing after things for the rest of your life in the vein of hoping to find your worth."

I find it easiest to think about the concept of detachment in terms of appearance. When I first learned of this concept, I asked myself: *What would I do if I became disabled or disfigured like many of the patients I have cared for?* Seeing myself as an attractive, young woman, would it bother me if people no longer paid me compliments? How would I handle the inevitable loss of my own form? Looking back, these questions foreshadowed my biggest lesson in detachment: a cancer diagnosis.

During the time when I lived off the high of being a new physician, my body was already breaking. Something foreign was inside me: a tumor slowly growing and overtaking my optic nerve. When it manifested as issues at work (fatigue, lack of focus, burnout) and at home (infertility, marital strife, depression), I developed a deep self-hatred. Why was I having so much trouble in residency when all my colleagues seemed to be doing fine? Why was I the weak one? I was stuck in my ego and blind to what was happening around me.

However, with the dramatic diagnosis came detachment. Despite the uncertainty of what was ahead for me, I was overcome with gratitude.

I'm so grateful I found out what was causing me to feel so bad for so long.

I'm so grateful it wasn't a deadly kind of tumor.

I'm so grateful my cancer can be cured with surgery alone.

I'm so grateful medical technology exists that allow me to continue living and to become a mother without a pituitary gland.

You can start to detach from your ego by practicing three things: gratitude, self-compassion, and mindfulness. Remind yourself of what you're grateful for when you're struggling, but don't forget to do it when things are going well, too. Accept yourself as you are in the present moment; it is perfectly okay to accept and yet still want to change your circumstances. Finally, let go of past and future thinking to help you separate from your ego and recognize your inherent joy and creativity—much needed elements for designing your life.

YOUR AUTHENTIC SELF

I used to have a vast closet full of clothes. I spent hours poring over the trends in fashion magazines, and I lived for the thrill of shopping. We even built a huge walk-in closet space when we expanded our basement. There sat rows of embellished sweaters, pencil skirts, and beautiful silk dresses. In the middle of the closet was a set of open pull-out shelves where I displayed my 50+ pairs of shoes, many of them beautiful sculptures with heels and sparkles.

One day while standing in the center of the closet, I realized that many of my shoes were out of place, collecting dust next to other fancy clothes I might have only worn once or twice. I was an anesthesiologist after all, a profession that requires wearing a uniform of mere pajamas. I was a rock climber and a yogi who had lived in RVs, vans, and huts in Nepal. At this stage, most of my nonworking time was filled with joyful family moments, getting to know my new baby, and exercising. Why did I need all those skirts and heels for a life I didn't lead? I wanted to love them, but when I wore them, they just felt uncomfortable … forced.

Living an inauthentic life is like trying to navigate your day in a confining skirt and pointy-toed stilettos, when all you

really want deep down is to wear your most broken-in jeans
and a pair of soft sneakers. On my path to leaning out, I let go
of the fashionable image I thought I wanted for something
simpler and downsized.

Later that year, we moved to another home that had regular,
sliding door closets, and I got rid of all that stuff. A few years
after that, we lived in a small, two-bedroom condo before we
purchased our dream mountain property where we live
today, which so far only has a tiny house on wheels and no
closet. All my clothes now fit in small piles on one shelf.

What kind of shoes are you allowing yourself to wear right
now? Do they fit the life you really want to lead? It's fine to
appreciate and wear fancy shoes, but are you choosing them
for yourself, or is someone else choosing them for you?

AUTHENTICITY VS. PROFESSIONALISM

Some elements of *Lean In* culture reek of inauthenticity, particularly saying "yes" to all opportunities and ignoring any
nagging voices with urgings to lean out. If you are accepting
the status quo because you think you should or because you
believe you don't have the abilities to do anything different,
you are not being your authentic self. If you are living by
others' definitions of success, wellness, and balance, you are
not living your authentic life. Authenticity is at the root of
happiness, creativity, and productivity; pretending to be
someone else while you're at work is a recipe for burnout and
stress-related illness.

In addition, if you are chasing perfectionism and upholding
an image of invulnerability, you are living inauthentically. We
walk the line of being professional, which requires some level
of detachment from emotion to perform objectively, and
sharing our humanness with our patients, clients, and other
coworkers. Instead of adhering to a rigid standard, it should

be up to each person to decide how to navigate that line. Showing even just a sliver of your humanity at work is the first step toward changing this culture.

In my investigation of women physicians' experiences navigating infertility treatments while working, many of them commented that they regretted keeping their treatments a secret. A few even mentioned being reprimanded by superiors for requesting vacation without adequate notice or taking "unplanned absences."[3] A surgeon recounted her experience operating on a long workday while actively miscarrying. This kind of inauthenticity adds more stress to an already stressful situation, and it prevents better, more human-centered policymaking at work.

Ironically, as mentioned previously, research shows that when we reveal vulnerable parts of ourselves to others, it increases our likability.[4] To find your authenticity, return to your values. Psychologist Adam Grant said, "Being genuine is closing the gap between what you value and what you express."

Lastly, your authentic self is most invested in your greatest asset: *you*. Your authentic self *wants* to invest in you—to find purpose, clarify values, stay active and well, and identify sustainable habits of self-care. Your authentic self thinks critically about the situation and openly wonders if there is a better option. Your authentic self knows what's most important.

BE YOU

Being "who you are" at both work and home bucks the tradition in a much-needed way. It fosters agency, which is a key factor for preventing burnout. It draws out the authenticity in others. It endears others toward your endeavors, whatever "beautiful mess" they might make. When you are authentic, people will sense the positive energy in you; they will want to help you and cheer you on.

"Who you are" will become your guiding light through the uncertainty of leaning out.

EXERCISE: CHILDHOOD PICTURE VISUALIZATION

(Adapted from a mental fitness training exercise by Shirzad Chamine, founder of Positive Intelligence[5])

Find a picture of yourself, either in print or digital format. Some of us had a happy childhood, while some of us had a not-so-happy childhood. If there has been trauma in your past, please don't take yourself to a scene of trauma. Try to find a moment of joy and happiness in your memories of childhood. If you cannot think of one, make up a scene with you as a happy child.

Sit in a comfortable position and focus on your breath for a couple of minutes. When you're ready, take a look at your childhood picture. Now envision a scene from your past where you are a happy child ... sometime in your life before age 10. Notice what is happening in this scene. Notice who's there, what the environment is like, what expression you have on your face ... notice as many details as you can.

See yourself as your original, true self—the beautiful being you were intended to be. Choose some words or adjectives that describe the beautiful being in this scene.

Notice how this being is worthy of all the unconditional love in the world. Notice that this being does not need to earn love, does not need to work for love, does not need to prove anything. This being is worthy just as she is.

This is who you really are.

And you get to give this being the love she deserves. Only you, as the adult you are now, can give that kind of unconditional love to yourself. This being has always deserved it, but she might not have necessarily received it. And you get to begin to do that now. Notice how beautiful this being is. Notice how worthy of unconditional love this being is.

This is the unchanging you. This is the true you. You're a special being, and you get to remember who you are.

MARGOT'S JOURNEY

"Everybody has to find their own path, but I wish I'd had more confidence in my own voice earlier."

Margot grew up traveling the world with her family. As a young woman, she developed her own core values of adventure and curiosity for experiencing new things. At the same time, her midwestern Arkansas upbringing deeply instilled in her the importance of community and relationships.

That sense of adventure led her to big city life after law school. Margot wanted to experience the big city, but she didn't want necessarily want the life of Big Law. "I never wanted to work for the big corporate firm, to be a cog in that wheel," she said.

Knowing that she desired closer client relationships, she chose a small, boutique law firm as her first professional workplace. After shifting to another boutique firm a couple years later, she realized that what she was doing wasn't much different than the big firms—except for the salary.

When Margot was approached about her intentions for partnership, she realized she "really wanted to be in a smaller community, have a more balanced work-life situation, and move to a place where I could have a house and a dog." She decided to take a gap year in search of the perfect small town that checked all her boxes.

Margot was no stranger to taking gap years. During college, she had spent a year traveling to Africa and working at Epcot Center in Florida. Between college and law school, she spent several months in Australia. Having positioned many different "sabbaticals" into my own life since college (sometimes to the dismay of others), Margot is a woman after my own heart.

During Margot's most recent gap year, she spent time in Thailand before setting off on a Western states quest to find her perfect mountain town. She settled on Bozeman, which offered good outdoor and work opportunities, was affordable, and had a college. Check, check, and check. She found a job with a local small firm by simply contacting all the practicing attorneys in the area and asking to talk to them about what it was like to practice there.

Did she receive any pushback about the gaps on her resume? "No. Only one person was skeptical that I would like it enough to keep living here," she said. There were no questions about her skills or lost work time.

Not only did moving to a small town help Margot develop the closer relationships with clients that she craved, she also quickly formed a network of professional women friends. Through one of them, she met her husband. When they got married, she was in her late 30s. Luckily, she was able to have one child at age 40 without the help of infertility treatments. "I know many women who have struggled," she said.

Motherhood challenged Margot to again rethink what she wanted out of her law career. Although she loved the clients she had developed, she desired more control over her schedule. Little by little, she began to transition her case load from litigation to transactional. Then, she opened her own firm.

Today, Margot continues to value her client relationships in a solo practice that offers complete control and portability. When her mother broke her hip and needed help with home rehabilitation, Margot was able to make the cross-country drive with her son (on summer break from school) to help with the rehabilitation process … while still tending to client matters. "None of them really knew the difference. Thank goodness I had that flexibility," she said.

When asked what advice she'd give to other attorneys stuck on the treadmill of achievement, Margot's advice is simple, but not necessarily easy:

"Find your own path. Figure out what brings you joy. Build relationships."

CHAPTER 7
SELF-KNOWLEDGE IS A SUPERPOWER

"I don't even remember what I enjoy doing."

"I can't relax and just be at home anymore."

"I don't know who I really am."

Do any of these statements sound familiar? How would you answer if I asked you what you liked to do for fun? I've heard these kinds of sentiments numerous times, especially from professional women who've added parenting into the mix. Not only have these women had their heads down, running on the treadmill of achievement for so long that they've forgotten these things, they've often given up a substantial amount of "me" time for years so they can support and raise little humans.

This one-two punch leaves women in a state where they're used to taking care of everything and everyone—except themselves. Fellow physician, author, and podcaster Errin Weisman, DO, said, "My life had been so consumed with achieving, doing unpaid work, looking after my kids, and stressing about everything else that I had stopped doing anything *just for fun*."

Taking some time to learn about or rediscover yourself is of utmost value on your journey to leaning out. Businesswoman and fashion designer Diane von Furstenberg said, "The most powerful relationship you will have is the relationship with yourself." In fact, self-knowledge helps to increase happiness, enhance success, and optimize habits. If you don't know yourself well, you are more apt to be influenced by external forces (such as the strong ones that come with the *Lean In* culture) and less likely to stay true to your values.

How do you go about increasing self-knowledge? It starts by making a priority to spend time with yourself.

GO SOLO

Time alone affords you the space to both be reflective and mindful. Many people feel that when they're down or stressed, the best thing to do is surround themselves with friends and family (perhaps with a numbing out ceremony involving rich food and alcohol), yet time alone is valuable— even for extroverts. Alone time does not have to be lonely. It helps you examine the constant chatter in your head and clarify your thoughts and feelings.

In keeping with the high achiever's penchant for all-or-nothing thinking, it's tempting to believe that you have no time for alone time unless you can escape to a spa retreat for the weekend. The reality is that alone time can be long and luxurious, or it can be short and simple. If it's the latter, find a way to make it frequent; every minute adds up. Can you take a short walk by yourself sometime during the day? Is there a period of even 10 minutes when you can sit quietly alone?

An often-undervalued source of alone time is the workday commute. It's an easy way to savor even just a few minutes of alone time. Most people spend their commutes either listening to the news, talking on the phone, blaring the radio, or doing more work (!) if they use public transit. You already spend the time commuting anyway, so why not make it productive—not in an achievement sort of way, but as a manner of increasing your self-awareness?

I prefer to use my commutes as an opportunity for silence. When I commuted regularly, I commonly used the time to either perform a breathing exercise or a meditation. (More on both in Chapter 9.) I would then use the drive home to reflect on the day. *What went well today? What did I learn? What did I really enjoy about today?*

Journaling is a great way to reflect on your life during your alone time. If you don't like to write or you prefer to spend alone time walking, you can dictate your journal. Write or dictate the happenings today that made you smile. What aspects of your day did you really enjoy, and how did you *feel* while they were happening? Alternately, you can also reflect on what parts of your day you disliked.

When you do this on a regular basis, you will begin to see patterns. You will recognize the elements of your work and life that are continually filling your cup. At the same time, you'll identify the draining elements you'd really like to remove.

CULTIVATE SELF-COMPASSION

Another foundational element of self-knowledge is self-compassion, yet it is especially elusive for high-achieving givers. Both *Lean In* culture and Western family culture emphasize putting others' needs and desires above our own. Thus, self-care and self-compassion are often considered selfish and indulgent. Self-compassion is also associated with settling for less, which goes against the beliefs of those stuck on the treadmill of achievement. At the heart of the perfectionism and comparison many of us experience is a lack of self-compassion.

It's time to challenge these beliefs. Psychologist and self-compassion expert Kristin Neff, PhD, stresses that self-compassion involves three elements, each of which is commonly accepted on its own merit: kindness, mindfulness, and a sense of connection to the human experience.[1] How would you treat a friend, family member, client, or patient who comes to you with negative self-talk? Can you acknowledge that whatever limiting beliefs and negative feelings you're experiencing are common, natural, and yet fleeting? When you notice yourself using the thought traps outlined in Chapter 5 or bringing up excuses as to why you are stuck in your current work-life balance, notice your level of self-compassion. You do not need to treat yourself poorly while still showing up for everyone else. Author and spiritual teacher Jack Kornfield said, "If your compassion does not include yourself, it is incomplete."

ASSESSMENTS

Sometimes referred to as "personality tests," assessments can be another, very helpful way to increase self-knowledge. In the worst-case scenario, an assessment tells you something you already knew about yourself after you've invested some time (and possibly a little money). On the flip side, assessments can really illuminate certain traits you've never realized about yourself through objective, neutral questioning.

In my writing, speaking, and coaching, I have researched and taken many of these assessments. The following list includes my choices for maximum yield of insight with minimal investment.

Introvert vs. Extrovert

You might think you know what these terms mean, and you may have already characterized yourself as one or the other. Before you skip to the next section, consider taking Susan Cain's quiz[2], adapted from her book *Quiet: The Power of Introverts in a World That Can't Stop Talking*. Cain posits that the key to understanding if you're introverted or extroverted is *energy*. Social interactions and inputs tend to drain energy from people who are introverted, while extroverts will thrive and gain energy in the same situations. This piece of information is a cornerstone of self-care. If you continue living a life that has all the features of the type that isn't you, it's bound to leave you drained, burned out, and not creative. That doesn't mean you need to switch careers, however. You simply need to be smarter about your self-care time.

The Four Tendencies

When writing *Better Than Before*, author and happiness expert Gretchen Rubin (*The Happiness Project, Happier at Home*) researched strategies to get habits to stick. In doing so, she came up with the Four Tendencies framework, now the subject of a subsequent book titled *The Four Tendencies*. When conducting her many interviews, she realized that all personalities fall into four basic categories when it comes to how they respond to *expectation*s: Upholders, Questioners, Obligers, and Rebels. Your Tendency tells you whether you generally embrace or resist expectations, both those you have for yourself and those others place on you.

At last count, more than three million people have taken the quiz.[3] Your tendency affects how you adopt, maintain, and drop habits, which means that certain strategies for developing or quitting habits will work for specific tendencies. The results of this quiz can inform so much about your behavior around decisions, setting and achieve goals, and even how you relate to others in your household and workplace. Physicians and other professionals have also found it useful for their patient and client interactions.

The Five Love Languages

- Flowers
- A quiet night at home
- A foot massage
- A love note
- Having your drycleaning picked up

Which of these expressions of love appeals most to you? How do you tend to show your love to others?

The Five Love Languages are Words of Affirmation, Quality Time, Physical Touch, Giving/Receiving Gifts, and Acts of Service. The book and corresponding assessment[4] were originally developed for family counseling. It sounds like this assessment is unrelated to the goal of increasing self-awareness, but knowing your Love Language can help you beyond your romantic relationships. It will help you navigate *all* relationships, including the most important one—the one you have with yourself.

How you prefer to give and receive affection is key for understanding your and others' actions, but it can also provide insight into developing the most effective self-care practices for you. For example, a Words of Affirmation person can use journals, books, and mantra meditations when they need to clear their thoughts. If you prefer Quality Time, you can be sure to recharge by spending even a little time alone. People who gravitate toward Physical Touch can turn to massage, yoga, or simply enveloping themselves in a soft, warm blanket when they need self-care. A Gifts person could buy themselves flowers or cook a lavish dinner when they're feeling down. And finally, if Service fills your cup, you can hire someone to clean your house or make an effort to schedule a much-needed doctor appointment.

Four other assessments you might be familiar with from workplace trainings or coaching resources are the Myers-Briggs Type Inventory, the Enneagram, the Big Five Personality Assessment, and the CliftonStrengths Assessment. Myers-Briggs types were developed to help people understand their preferences in various work and home scenarios. The Enneagram numbers one through nine are used to characterize behaviors, motivations, and fears. The Big Five represent dimensions of all personalities in differing extents—extroversion, agreeableness, openness, conscientiousness, and neuroticism. Finally, CliftonStrengths is designed to elucidate your leadership style.

There are more assessments available, but the ones listed in this section are my favorites. The ones I discussed in detail above are quick, free, and do not require the help of a coach or psychologist to interpret the results. Links and resources for all these assessments are provided in the Resources section at the end of this book.

THE GIFT OF SELF-KNOWLEDGE

Above all, self-knowledge will bring you clarity. It will help you get in touch with your deeply held values. It will improve your relationships at work and at home. It will enhance your productivity and habits. There is not a one-size-fits-all solution to deal with the problems of *Lean In* culture. Self-knowledge will help you see solutions that are right for you, so you can design your journey of leaning out from a place of internal value, rather than crowdsourcing solutions that might lead to not-so-lasting change.

EXERCISE: LEARN SOMETHING NEW ABOUT YOURSELF

Choose one of the assessments that appeals to you from the descriptions above. Take the assessment and then reflect on the results. How does this change your view of yourself? Does what you've learned align with your roles and the types of activities that currently fill your days?

SARA'S JOURNEY

"I know myself pretty well."

Sara grew up quickly because her father traveled for work most of the time. She and her siblings were forced to take care of her mother, who was debilitated from a severe case of multiple sclerosis. "No judgement … but I knew I did not want to be like my dad," she said. "I knew I wanted to be able to take care of my family financially on my terms and still be around … and not have to be subject to someone else's idea of how long I have to be at work."

During college, she dated a man who planned to follow in his father's footsteps and become a chiropractor. Although she held a vision of balancing work and children, Sara didn't know where she wanted to focus her studies. One day, her boyfriend's dad said, "You're really good with numbers; you should be an accountant." She dismissed this, thinking it sounded boring … until he added, "With the right credentials, you could be working by a pool someday."

Already armed with the knowledge of her core values, that was the moment she began designing her authentic work-life balance. Furthermore, she married that boyfriend. They now have two young children, and she owns her own business as a CPA. Her current work schedule is comprised of three afternoons per week in an office with one assistant, seeing clients both in person and virtually. She also teaches two virtual courses at the same local university where she attended school and met her husband. The rest of her days are filled with family time, gardening, and focusing on her own health and fitness, both outdoors and in a gym.

Sara chose to attend a virtual graduate school that helped her earn three master's degrees and her public accountant certification. Thus, she stayed focused on her goal of complete schedule control without the distraction of comparison to her peers. However, her first CPA job out of school involved tremendous work hours, especially during tax season. "Within six months, they had started grooming me to become a partner," she said. Although she welcomed the experience as something to try for one tax season, it gave her even more confirmation that her original vision was the right path for her. "It's just not that time of life for me," she said.

When she and her husband left that environment, they both started their own businesses at the same time. "We had no guaranteed income," she said. They continued to live below their means and focus their efforts on the things that mattered most to them: carving out niches in their fields that were amenable to part-time hours and focusing on family. Neither of them care about fancy things or lifestyle upgrades.

As part of her journey, Sara has learned a tremendous amount about being a solopreneur. During periods of financial uncertainty, "I said yes to every job that came my way." Over time, "it took a little bit to learn to say no." She honed her small boutique practice by raising prices and developing a sense of which potential clients would demonstrate the level of professionalism that she wanted. "I get that desire to do more… I don't scroll through Facebook, I scroll through Indeed and look at the jobs," she said. But she stays true to her practice by remembering what matters most to her—her family. "This time of life seems like the time for raising kids."

Sara is an example of someone who has remained focused on her own vision of work-life balance because, through adversity, she developed deep self-knowledge at an early age. However, the one thing she wishes she knew as the young girl caring for her ill mother was to cultivate a growth mindset. "I grew up with [the mentality that] 'life is just the way it is,' but I've learned that you go create your life," Sara said.

CHAPTER 8
REDEFINING SUCCESS

"Success is liking yourself, liking what you do, and liking how you do it."—Maya Angelou

For many, success is comprised of two main metrics: salary and job title. Possessions are often included as well. The reality is there are infinite ways to define success, on both a macro and micro level. You can define success by what is most important to you. Is it based on being in a loving marriage? Having the means to travel wherever you want to go? Making an impact in your career field? Feeling a deep spiritual connection? Adding value to a community?

Similar to how the self is not physical attributes, accomplishments, or titles (see Chapter 6), success is definitely:

- *Not linear:* Rarely does success in any pursuit come without some amount of failure. Setbacks, plateaus, and slow patches are easy to identify in pursuits like sports, but for some reason, we often expect our work lives to resemble a steady, linear climb. Even Sheryl Sandberg noted in *Lean In* that "careers are a jungle gym, not a ladder."

- *Not brutal:* If your idea of success includes suffering and beating yourself up in the process, you need to leave behind the martyr mindset that's so deeply ingrained in the *Lean In* culture. Most people will agree that good health is at the foundation of everything we might want to do. Thus, true success cannot come at the cost of wellbeing and self-care time.
- *Not serious:* Life journeys should involve some aspect of fun (even if it's "type II fun"). Are you successful if you're not enjoying what you're doing? Ask a typical doctor, lawyer, or other hard-driving professional what they do for fun, and you might get a blank stare. Yet these are the people who are traditionally thought of as "successful."
- *Not absolute:* Any woman who would have the interest to pick up this book should recognize that she is already in the top 1 percent of how most people define success. Success is relative to the observer, is a moving target, and should be constantly redefined based on circumstances.

I like to envision success as a circular pie with many slices. All the slices are different sizes; Health might be a very large chunk of the pie, while having a sense of Purpose also takes up a big piece. Salary and Job Title make up diet-sized slivers. I'm not even sure Stuff deserves a piece of the pie. Additional pieces might represent Relationships, Finances, or other things. It all depends on what you really value.

IDENTIFYING YOUR VALUES

Your values lie at the heart of your definition of success. When most people think about values, images of church or family come to mind. However, values are much more than beliefs about **morality**. Values are root principles that guide our actions and behaviors in a wide range of circumstances. Examples include autonomy, creativity, and health.

The concept of values is quite simple, but identifying and consistently living by them might not be easy. In a word or two, they represent what we each consider to be most important. Values can change over time based on life's different seasons, but they tend to be fairly constant principles. They form an internal compass that affects both everyday decisions and long-term directions.

You can find many lists of values online, but I've included one in the Resources section of this book. You can also find clues to your values by asking yourself some questions. What kinds of relationships do you have and want in your life? What inspires you? If you had infinite money and resources, what would you do? What do you want to be known for? What pulls at your heartstrings?

FORGET COMPARISON

Through his social science research on high achievers, author and professor Arthur C. Brooks has realized that outwardly successful people often continue the patterns that earned them success while inadvertently detracting from their own happiness. He talked of interviewing a very successful businesswoman, who admitted to having a loveless marriage, empty relationships with her adult children, newly diagnosed health problems, and poor sleep.[1] He asked her why, as a billionaire CEO of her own company, she doesn't fix those problems by changing her schedule to make them a priority. After a moment of thought, she said, "I guess I'd prefer to be special than happy." This is success addiction and ultimate entrenchment on the treadmill of achievement.

These hidden costs often occur behind the scenes, the glossy social media photos, and curated posts. Why compare yourself to this? If you agree with my assertion that there are many different definitions of success, why would you compare how you're doing to others? When we base success on intrinsic factors like self-identified values, we avoid the comparison trap of the "worldly" success metrics: money, power, and recognition.

Eleanor Roosevelt said, "No one can make you feel inferior without your consent." If you believe you're successful and are clear on how you define it, you will also avoid measuring yourself against others.

THE CHANGING SEASONS

In the middle of my residency, I had my first coaching experience. I met my coach when I was seriously ill and didn't know it yet, questioning why I had chosen to upend my life and pursue medicine. He was an executive coach and was married to my faculty mentor; she graciously arranged for us to work together for a few sessions.

Due to his relationship to one of my superiors, I initially hid my burnout and intermittent thoughts of quitting altogether to become a Starbucks barista. Instead, I flooded him with all sorts of conflicting ideas: What do I *really* want to do when I finish residency? I was already doubting the highly specialized path of preoperative echocardiography I had jumped on. I knew I wanted my work life to have vast variety, with a mix of patient care, writing, speaking, and other things not yet identified.

All the overwhelm and confusion paralyzed me. Should I pivot entirely and work in a pain clinic? What about just going into private practice? How about nonclinical pursuits? What about my other loves: my marriage (which was suffering), travel, and rock climbing? When would I be able to focus on them again? And when would I be able to have a child?

My coach looked at me with a smile and said, "You can do all these things, but you can't reasonably focus on them all at the same time."

This was mind-blowing. Up until then, I had an idea in my head that all the successful people I saw around me just hammered at all their endeavors. Maybe some of them do … but not the ones who have sustainable, long-term happiness without dysfunctional relationships and burnout.

My coach had me construct a chart. I listed important time periods such as "now until graduation," "first two years out of residency," and "next five years" down the left column. Across the top, he had me write three headings:

FOCUS / / LET SLIDE / / IGNORE ALTOGETHER

I still use this exercise with my own coaching clients, and I pull it out when I'm personally feeling overwhelmed.

Work-life balance changes with different seasons of your life. One season, you're ramping up a business from scratch, learning a new technology, or completing intensive training in your profession. Social obligations will likely drop off your priority list. The next season might be the year of relationships, where you focus more on your marriage or perhaps an ill loved one you must care for. Another season might be the time to place hard boundaries at work so you can focus on supporting your children's passions. Yet another season might be the time to prioritize your own wellness by setting meeting times in pen with a personal trainer, investing in a yoga meditation retreat, or carving out time every week to prepare your own fresh meals.

Very few things in life, besides our age in years, progress as an upward climb toward a pinnacle. Yet for some reason, we often assume that's the way things will go. As years go by, you'll steadily make more and more money. If you consistently work out in the gym, you'll just keep getting stronger. The reality is that progress in any pursuit ebbs and flows. Thus, our definition of success can also change with the seasons.

AUTHENTIC LEADERSHIP

In *Lean In*, Sheryl Sandberg argued that if more women were in leadership positions, better work-life balance policies would exist for all of us. The dream of "better policies" is a nice one, but the key need is flexibility for individuals. Flexibility will only proliferate in the workplace when women step up as *authentic leaders*.

Traditional leaders command corner offices, make policies, and supervise large teams, but there is also the kind of leader who empowers others merely by setting an example. This is an *authentic leader*—a person who shows others that it's okay to be human, that boundaries are a gift to herself and others, that forging a new path is possible. She embodies the John Quincy Adams quote: "If your actions inspire others to dream more, learn more, do more, and become more, you are a leader."

An authentic leader also welcomes different visions of work fulfillment and balance, knowing that her definitions might not resonate with others. She fiercely aligns with her personal vision but accepts the diverse views of others.

This is the kind of leadership that will change the culture of hustle and invulnerability.

She courageously steps away from the status quo and demonstrates for others that it's possible. She is leading by example.

EXERCISE: WHAT ARE YOUR CORE VALUES?

This exercise is very simple, yet it takes some time and iterative examination to complete. Look at the list of values included in the Resources section. Which words speak to you? Write 10 of these words on a separate paper. This is your working list. On a different day, revisit your list. On another day, narrow your list to five words. Can you narrow the list even further? Having three to five core values is a great place to be.

CHERI'S JOURNEY

"Oh ... I'm leaning WAY out."

That is what Cheri replied when I asked if she would be featured in this book, and she wasn't kidding. Cheri goes by two distinct names: Dr. (Maiden Name) and Mrs. (Married Name). For almost 15 years, she was solely known as the former while working as a full-time physiatrist and breadwinner for her family in a moderately sized mountain town.

After a conflict over compensation for clinical services, she left her hospital-based small group to work at a skilled nursing facility. Again, when leadership experienced an upheaval, "I knew there would be changes coming, so I started looking for other options." She transitioned to travel-only work as a *locum tenens* physiatrist, which took her all over the country for her assignments.

When COVID hit, "my work evaporated overnight," she said. At the same time, she noticed that she really enjoyed being home with her family more than she thought she would. Her two daughters were entering their teens: a difficult time for a parent to be away. When an opportunity to fill a position as a long-term substitute math teacher came up at her daughters' school, she said yes.

This was not an immediate "Hell yes;" in fact, she wasn't so sure she'd like teaching. Her husband thought she was crazy for doing it, but she decided it would be a fun experiment. She completed another long-term assignment as an English teacher and now works as a regular sub for the school. In addition, she coaches the cross-country team and started the school's first personal finance club.

Now that *locum* work has ramped up again nationwide, Cheri travels for a few clinical assignments here and there. She also performs disability evaluations for the US Department of Veterans Affairs and expert witness work for a couple of loyal law firms. In addition, she and her husband own a couple of small businesses and real estate investments.

On the surface, it seems like Cheri's got her hands full. "I did not think I had it in me to be *that mom*," she said of her transformation from being known as "Dr." to "Mrs." She does not carry reservations about frequently putting her role as a physician aside. "In medicine, we learn to talk to lots of different people; we learn to hold space for people." She's doing that now as a mentor to teenagers in her local town.

How has Cheri been able to embrace so much uncertainty and try entrepreneurial ventures, different medical business models, and even substitute teaching as part of her journey? "I immersed myself in the FI (Financial Independence) space between 2009 and 2012," she said. By following early FI bloggers JD Roth of Get Rich Slowly and Pete of Mr. Money Mustache, she gained inspiration that it was possible to embrace minimalism and find financial freedom. She also found camaraderie and advice from the nationwide FI community at conferences and retreats, which she continues to attend yearly.

On navigating financial uncertainty, Cheri advises other women wanting to lean out that, "Money is only the most important thing if you don't have enough of it." She encourages other women to recognize what "enough" means for them; they have the ability to live on less if necessary to get the life they want. "You have a skillset. You are already resilient."

For as long as I've known her, Cheri has designed her life through experimentation. She's been a part of multiple small business ventures, including her husband's BASE jumping guide business and a lactation cookie company. While she continues to wonder if she's finally found "her thing"—her calling, her purpose—she's never been happier with her current blend of teaching, clinical work, mentoring, and being a mom. "Ten years ago, I was so unhappy. I felt like I was drowning," she said. "This has been so much fun! I'm so much happier than when I was in the hospital every day."

CHAPTER 9
DOING HARD THINGS

"You don't need confidence to pursue a challenging goal. You build your confidence through pursuing challenging goals." —Adam Grant

Willa* is an architect and the breadwinner of her family. Her children have lived their entire lives in their suburban home on a busy street of a relatively large city. Over the years, they've grown tired of their lack of ability to move about in their own yard, let alone their neighborhood. The kids don't feel safe playing outside anymore. They've had one break-in, and on another occasion, a brick came flying through their front window while they were eating dinner.

After my family and I moved to the mountains, she and her family came to stay for a weekend. The children loved frolicking in the stream, hunting for horny toads, and running on dirt roads where no cars ever drive. Willa and her husband sat in our Adirondack chairs, peered up at the hundred-foot-tall pines, and both sighed. The forest environment brought back childhood memories for each of them. I could see the wheels turning.

While they couldn't wrap their heads around the idea of living off grid an hour from civilization and six miles down a dirt road like we do, they fell in love with a nearby small town. They casually began researching homes in the area ... then they traveled to see some. There was only one big wrinkle: Willa loves her job at the big city design firm, and the CEO had recently placed a moratorium on remote work positions.

It would be glorious if situations like this, the ones that become tied to a decision we can't un-envision, came and went without drama or difficulty. Instead, leaning out often involves big conflict and uncertainty. Sacrifice and discomfort are inevitable. The good news is you can "train" yourself to handle anything difficult that comes your way on this journey!

High achievers are, by definition, strong and resilient. You have done and can already do hard things, and this begets doing *more* hard things. Doing hard things of any type will give you confidence. It will also open your brain to more creative thinking. As author and speaker Jen Sincero said, "Obstacles and challenges are the agents of growth."

There are a few principles about "hard" to get clear first. Hard is relative, so your specific level of hard will be different from someone else's. Also, hard can mean many different things. Hard can be technically difficult, uncomfortable, scary, or awkward. It can also mean new, awe-inspiring, amazing, and creative.

Below are thoughts and information on different types of hard things. Try experimenting with some of these in low-stakes situations, and if you recognize that you've already done work in some of these areas, give yourself credit for cultivating courage.

TRY SOMETHING NEW

Confidence is an elusive quality we all crave: confidence to ask for what you want, to take your own path to sustainable work-life balance, to seize opportunities when they present themselves. True confidence is knowing that you can experience any feeling or emotion—whether it's fear, love, or anything in between. Psychologist Susan David, PhD describes this as "emotional agility."[1] What better way is there to test emotional agility than to simply try something new?

As creatures of comfort and habit, trying something new is the quintessential "hard thing." Newness can help you get into a flow state, and it can foster growth and joy. Trying new things helps achievement-addicted people learn to separate their worth from their achievements and/or failures. If it's new, what do you have to lose?

Start with something small and fun. Consider taking a class about a subject you've always wanted to learn, such as an art, a craft, an instrument, or a new fitness class. Try making a food dish you've never eaten in your life. Travel to a place you've never been, with no itinerary other than simple exploration. Or just make an effort to take a different route between work and home or to other places you frequently go.

If you have trouble fitting something new into your routine, identify ways to increase your accountability. Consider hiring a coach or joining a team organization. Volunteer to give a presentation to a group of people (if this is not something you do as part of your regular work). Novelty can bring about exhilaration, reticence, or anything in between. Experiment with new things that let you *feel* on both sides. Work up to leaning out by increasing the intensity of the new things you try.

LEARN TO REST

If you watch an elite rock climber scale a challenging cliff face, solving the riddle of sequences to reach the top without falling, it might take a while. It might even get a little boring because she will take rests wherever she can find them. A shake of the hand here, a heel hook on the rock there … rests are key steps in her journey to the top. The same goes for powerlifters. In between their attempts at lifting heavier and heavier weight, it is often imperative that they rest for several minutes.

Athletes know that rest is integral to high performance. Without rest, the body will not cooperate with progression. At worst, it might become injured or ill. Journalist and digital entrepreneur Arianna Huffington collapsed from lack of sleep and exhaustion in 2007, suffering facial fractures from the fall. She made it her mission to overhaul her personal sleep and rest habits—and also to change the culture of insomniac corporate automatons. "For the human operating system, downtime is not a bug. It's a feature," she said.[2] She even wrote a book about the subject in 2015 called *Thrive*.

Despite more attention from mainstream media such as *Wallstreet Journal* and *Harvard Business Review*, adequate rest is still elusive for many professionals. How many of us say, "I'll rest when I'm done with _____" instead of prioritizing rest as we go? According to Greg McKeown, author of *Essentialism*, rest is absolutely essential for everyone. Unfortunately, rest goes against the prevailing culture, and also it's a legitimately hard thing for many of us to do. We might resist rest out of virtue, but there are other sneaky reasons at play. Rest can feel lazy, indulgent, or impossible. Feelings of overwhelm and time scarcity might also contribute to the notion that we just can't rest.

A good rule of thumb: If you've been struggling but you don't know why or you're feeling overwhelmed and can't tell what you need, what you likely need is rest.

Rest can take many different forms. The most familiar type of rest is the physical kind—sleeping longer, taking naps, and skipping the gym when you're tired. But taking even small breaks throughout the day can restore motivation, creativity, and focus. Rest can also look like a break in the middle of the day or a moment of looking away from your screen to focus your eyes on something in the distance. Rest can look like stepping outside for a short walk around the building. When you spend hours inside under artificial lighting, the warmth of the sun on your face can feel like a luxurious, restful treat.

Maybe you need a few quiet moments to yourself to slow down your mind, or to escape from the feeling of needing to perform or be "on" all the time. Maybe you need a rest from difficult or inauthentic moments, to just *feel* your feelings. This kind of rest could look like escaping to a quiet room for a few minutes to be with yourself. If you can't physically get away in the moment, a useful thing to try is focusing on one or more of your senses acutely for a few minutes. You could rub your fingers or palms together, notice the weight of your feet on the floor, or pay exquisite attention to sights or sounds around you. This type of brain reset will short-circuit the pathways your brain usually takes toward triggering thoughts.

If you're struggling with burnout or feeling stuck, consider arranging a longer rest—a sabbatical. This could look like an official leave of 1 to 12 months in length. It can also simply mean taking advantage of an extended period of time between two jobs. I've taken both types of sabbaticals during my career, and each experience brought tremendous perspective and clarity.

Experiment with rests of different lengths and types. Allow the concept of rest to infiltrate your life and become part of the rule—rather than the exception. Like rock climbers, consider designing your life as a series of moves positioned between rests.

SPEND TIME IN NATURE

Making a priority to spend time outside is the next-level step to embracing rest. Being outside provides a much-needed break from work and other tasks, and it has also been shown to enhance time perception and overall wellbeing. A survey study found that when people experience the feeling of awe (accompanying such events as seeing the vast beauty of the Grand Canyon or witnessing a powerful thunderstorm), their perception of time shifts from scarcity to abundance.[3] I don't know any woman who wouldn't love a sense of more time in her day, so making a priority to get outside more is a worthy challenge.

Like mindfulness, rest, and anything you want to develop into a sustainable habit, consider taking regular small steps to spend more time outside. This can be as simple as parking further away from your workplace, so you enjoy a longer stroll into the building. If you can commute between work-places or other locations by foot or bike, this would be a great way to work both activity and outside time into your days.

Can you spend even a few hours on the weekend taking a walk with friends, loved ones, or family members? What "brown sign" attractions[4] can you visit near your home? Children love to explore new areas, and these are often free outside attractions to explore in your area. Camping is another option for people who have the means and time; an even better camping experience would be one with no connectivity for a day or a weekend.

STAY IN THE PRESENT MOMENT

Mindfulness: You know you want it. Everyone's talking about it. At the same time, living in the present moment is a difficult thing for our runaway minds to do. Experimenting with mindfulness techniques will help train you to be calm and centered while you do hard things. At the same time, it will also benefit you in other ways.

The benefits of mindfulness have been well studied. They include increased happiness, decreased anxiety, and decreased job burnout. There is also a negative association with the practice of mindfulness and the incidence of health issues such as heart disease, Alzheimer's disease, and chronic pain conditions. Mindfulness techniques run the gamut from a practice of noticing things around you to full blown transcendental meditation sessions.

The thing that makes mindfulness seem hard is our desire to do it perfectly. In reality, being mindful is something you'll never do perfectly. It's about cultivating a practice of noticing, observing, and letting go of thoughts. It is not about the complete absence of thought but instead about witnessing and releasing thoughts as they come.

One of the most common techniques to try is guided meditation. There are many apps available, both free and paid, that can assist with guided meditations. Spend a little time experimenting with some and see what you like. You can also do meditation on your own by simply sitting in silence for a specified period of time. It doesn't have to be long, and it can be increased slowly as you get used to the practice.

Breathwork is another approachable technique for mindfulness. Two breath patterns to experiment with are box breathing and 4-7-8 breathing. With box breathing, you inhale for a chosen number of counts and exhale for the same

number, repeating the process for as long as you wish. 4-7-8
breathing is championed by integrative physician Andrew
Weil, MD, and it has been shown to increase parasympathetic
(rest and digest) neural tone.[5] Find your own cadence for how
fast to count based on what feels right to you. Inhale for four
counts, hold the breath for seven counts, and exhale for eight
counts. I used to perform this breathing exercise in silence
every time I commuted to and from work; it's a perfect time
to experiment with breathing practices.

One of my favorite ways to cultivate mindfulness is through
the concept of mental fitness.[6] Rooted in the science of neuroplasticity, strengthening mental fitness means that you train
your brain to take new neuronal paths to achieve its connections, vs. the tired, stale paths your brain usually follows. The
exercises consist of focusing intently on one particular sense
—touch, vision, or hearing, for example. I described this
above in the Rest section as well. The beauty of this is that it
can be done in public and can make a difference in as little as
two to five minutes.

The key with mindfulness exercises is developing a consistent
habit of doing them. To reap the benefits, you need to do
them at least daily. However, the short exercises described
here are easy to complete one to three times a day.

MAKE DECISIONS

Indecision can stem from a lack of confidence and clarity in
what you really want. Aside from doing the deep self-inquiry
work discussed in Chapters 6 through 8, you can work up to
making bigger decisions by practicing small, deliberate ones.
In turn, you will develop self-trust and intuition.

You already make numerous decisions every day. Identify the
ones you take for granted, write them down, and celebrate
them. Reflect on them with gratitude. When a low-stakes

decision comes up, practice making it quickly. For example, give yourself a time limit to choose the restaurant or decide on the travel itinerary.

Every decision not made has a cost of inaction. Doing nothing feels like an impartial "hold position," but doing nothing is actually *something*. Practice identifying the cost of inaction when you feel unable to commit to any decision, whether it be what to cook for dinner or whether to leave a long-term job.

SAY NO

Saying yes to one thing means saying no to another, and that's the reality. We often don't consciously recognize the tradeoffs, yet tradeoffs are an important part of practicing balance. In my career, I have traded prestige and notoriety for a flexible, very part-time clinical schedule. I also trade late night TV time for more sleep, and six-pack abs for regular enjoyment of my favorite dark chocolate peanut butter cups.

It's very easy in our *Lean In* culture to assume that we must say yes to every opportunity, or there will be consequences. We'll disappoint important people. We'll miss out, and our career will take an unintended turn. When contemplating an answer of yes to any work opportunity, consider the tradeoffs to whatever is on the other side of your balance. Paulo Coelho, author of *The Alchenist*, said, "When you are saying 'yes' to others, make sure you are not saying 'no' to yourself."

From another perspective, saying no to more things that don't immediately light you up, things that don't align with your values, will leave you open for more meaningful yeses. You are not the only one who will benefit from less yeses and more no's. Your family, friends, and loved ones will experience positive tradeoffs, too.

If you're used to saying yes to everything, scenarios where you need to say no can invoke horrible feelings of guilt, worry, and dread. Look at saying no as an art that requires rehearsal and practice. Identify some low-stakes commitments where you can work on saying no: a social engagement, this month's book club, the purchase of another online course you won't complete. Learn and practice some creative ways to say no. Here are my favorites, inspired by ideas from Greg McKeown's *Essentialism*.[7]

Deferred No

This is the easiest way to start placing boundaries, and it's the tactic I use most often. I simply say, "I'm not sure; let me check with my [calendar] [husband] [etc.] and get back to you." Until I started doing this, I had no idea how many times I automatically said yes to things out of a mere inability to formulate a thoughtful response on the spot. Delaying a no helps to strengthen your reason and resolve.

In addition, if you have trouble with conflict (like I do), it's often easier to say no to someone when you're not right in front of them. An email or text is perfectly acceptable. It gives space between the ask and response, so you can think of the best words to use when you decline. You can craft your best response by journaling on it first or by asking a trusted friend or coach.

Soft No

Especially helpful when you must be face to face with the requester, a soft no is basically saying nothing. It's not saying yes, but it's not exactly saying no. Instead, you do one of two things: You either make an awkward silence and let the asker say the next thing, or you make a comment that is not an answer. It looks like, "That sounds like a unique opportunity… [silence]" If the need arises to give an answer on the spot, use the deferral techniques above.

Switcheroo No

Particularly effective in work situations, there are a couple different flavors of the switcheroo no. You can say, "Yes, I can make that a priority. What other role/project would you like me to eliminate/delegate?" This forces the asker to also consider their priorities. Another way this can work is by passing the ask to another person: "I'm unable to do that right now, but I'd highly suggest you check with ___ because that sounds like something they'd be really interested in." They don't have to know you suggested them, but if they find out, it's okay because it's complimentary to them (you think they would do a good job at the task) and yet not directly committing them to anything. The response now falls on them.

Policy No

This method works really well for small, generally impersonal social asks. Examples include, "I have a policy of not volunteering for more than one advisory board," or "I have a policy of not making donations over the telephone." While this no might seem curt, it's effective because it's universally understandable. Almost everyone has personal or family "policies" like this, whether they're aware of them or not, so people tend to respect the concept.

There are entire books written about the why and how of boundaries. If you want more information on this topic, my recommendations are listed in the Resources section.

GET HELP FROM OTHERS

For many summer seasons, I spent two to three days a week working on a rock climbing "project" (a process of mastering a challenging climbing route) in the Pipedream Cave. The cave is a vast amphitheater sitting in the aspen groves of central Utah, made up of multicolored cobblestones that are somehow glued together with little bits of sand. The easiest route in the cave gets a sturdy 5.10 grade, and the next route above that one is a tricky overhanging route in the mid-5.11 range. "Hard" is an accurate word to describe most of the climbing there, depending on your skill level.

I'd set my eye on a climbing route that I thought contained beautiful movement but was just out of my current ability to climb cleanly (with no mistakes or falls). Typically, a climber might try to climb a route "on sight" for the first time without looking to others for help, but if a section seems tricky or daunting, they ask other climbers who've climbed it before for "beta."

Beta—a climbing term that refers to advice, strategies, or ideas from others who've been there before you—is a concept I've always loved. Beta encourages you and opens your eyes to new ways of solving the problem in front of you. Sometimes the information or insights you receive from others don't work well *for you*, but beta always feels comforting. It alerts you to the reality that what you're doing is indeed challenging, yet others have figured out a way to do it for themselves.

Continuing with your head down and blinders on, persevering like a Lone Ranger, is a commonality of *Lean In* culture. Asking for help can be seen as a sign of weakness. Throughout your professional training and early career, you might have felt unsure and wanted guidance. You might have asked yourself, *"Is what I am needing obvious or stupid to other people?"* Sometimes, you need to do the hard thing of seeking help.

There is no shame in admitting when you could use a little beta.

Many conferences and retreats now cater to professional women, promising inspiration, empowerment, and camaraderie. Meeting other women who are going through similar career challenges can open your eyes to new possibilities for leaning out in your field, but you must do the hard thing of being open and vulnerable. One-on-one mentorship can also be helpful for specific problem solving, but you must do the hard thing of finding the right mentor.

Coaching is another type of help, like beta with a little magic thrown in. Coaching promotes self-discovery, self-reflection, and openness to possibilities so that you can become the best version of yourself. The relationship between coach and client is particularly non-hierarchical—unlike therapy, counseling, or mentorship. Coaching sessions are focused not on diagnoses or advice but instead on thoughts, goals, and feelings. Coaches offer support, tools, structure, accountability, and an objective sounding board for personal growth. In physician workplaces, coaching has also been proven to effectively increase quality of life, decrease burnout, improve job satisfaction, and foster resilience and engagement in careers.[8]

There are a couple of "hard things" about coaching. First, it requires a monetary investment you must make in yourself. One-on-one sessions, while more expensive, will give you the most bang for your buck in terms of personal insight and growth. They can range in price (at the time of publication) from $100 to $500 per session. Group coaching programs can be more economical, but they are less personal.

If you choose to try coaching, make sure to research your prospective coaches. While certifications and fancy trainings don't necessarily make a great coach, the key to a good coaching relationship is finding a reputable coach who has personal experience and/or experience coaching other professionals with the specific problem you're having.

Also, coaching requires you to *do work*. Unlike a mentor, a coach's role is not to give you advice but instead to ask

provocative questions and bring up different points of view
to draw out your own personal insights. Much like when one
rock climber gives beta to another, she is providing ideas from
her personal training and experience without offering an
exact solution. Each climber is different and must figure out
how to solve the riddle of climbing sequences to reach the
pinnacle of the route in a way that works for her body consti-
tution and strengths.

Coaching can seem like opening a pandora's box filled with
highly personal items from moments of your life, but for
many women (including me), it has proven to be a worth-
while investment of time, money, and vulnerability. I might
be biased, but I highly recommend it if you're having
conflicting feelings about leaning out.

LIVE ON LESS

There will be people who, despite a deep desire to lean out,
will dismiss it as something reserved for those who have
privilege and money. They will say they don't have choices
because they need their entire, full-time salary; they are
breadwinners, they have unique expenses like a special needs
child, etc. While these situations require consideration, you
are not trapped where you are. You always have choices, even
if you don't currently see them.

My lean out might have commenced with a health crisis, but
the journey to where I am now took time, sacrifice, and
courage. Consistently living below my means is the thread
that wove it all together. Having money saved and knowing
that I could easily live on less gave me added confidence to
ask for a reduced schedule at work after I had a baby. It later
enabled me to leave a steady job and collect the less stable
income of *locum tenens* work, a worthy sacrifice for the loca-

tion freedom I desired. It also helped me pursue my nonclinical business interests without worry about sunk costs or profit margins.

I've been asked, *"How do you afford your life? You must have* _____ *"* (fill in the blank with "real estate investments," "an inheritance," or "a husband who makes a lot of money.") In truth, my husband defected from the traditional law work environment to be a counterculture professional years before I did; he now works the amount he wants, when he wants. There is no secret formula to financial freedom. As mundane as it sounds, the secret is living simply and flexibly. It's about maximizing savings so that you can have what J.L. Collins calls F*ck You Money.[9]

Saving more and spending less is simple but by no means easy. If you know your core values, you can figure out ways to save. Take a nonjudgmental look at all your expenses. Are they aligned with your core values? If not, eliminate. You can do this swiftly or gradually, but no matter how you adjust, you'll feel more confident in your ability to live on less.

Professionals often finish their training with a high debt burden and years of loan repayments ahead of them. This does not preclude you from finding ways to live simply and to live on less. When you lean out, there is likely to be some financial uncertainty, but that won't always be the case. For now, keep your "why" for leaning out firmly planted in the forefront of your brain. Use it as your North Star.

DO THE THING

Years ago, I found the idea of meditation and stillness to be daunting, so I conducted my own 30-day challenge where I spent at least 10 minutes every day in silent meditation. Thirty days feels feasible to complete, and if you don't like the thing you're trying, you aren't committed for too long. At the same time, 30 days is long enough for a habit to become incorporated into your typical routine.

Choose a thing from the ideas presented in this chapter that seems hard for you. From what you choose, identify a single-item, achievable habit and set up a 30-day challenge. After the 30 days, reflect on how you felt, what you learned, and how you want to go forward with the habit.

To get back to Willa, she and her family ended up making the move. They gave up a rental property in their former city and compromised slightly on the size of their new home to live near a beautiful canyon on the edge of the small town. Her teenager is excited to find a local job, and they are all relishing their outdoor play time. More importantly, by leveraging her successful past projects and unique skills with a particular software program, Willa negotiated a "temporary" (yet indefinite) remote arrangement with her employer. In addition, the shakeup of her old situation expanded her ideas about working in design, and she is now investigating other remote opportunities.

EXERCISE: MAKE YOUR OWN PRIORITIES CHART

I discussed this idea in the previous chapter, but it also qualifies as a "hard thing," because—be honest—have you ever in your life "let anything slide"? Well, now's the time to figure out what you can let slide. Make your own chart as I described in Chapter 8. Keep your focus on the present time-frame and your current priorities. Imagine the future without judgement to fill in the other parts. Here are the three columns again.

FOCUS // LET SLIDE // IGNORE ALTOGETHER

KARA'S JOURNEY

"Once I made the decision, there was no turning back."

Kara is an ex-ballet dancer and internist in Atlanta. She spent 10 years working for a large, private practice group before the moment came that she knew she needed to lean out. She initially went through a serious bout of burnout, borne of her own perfectionist and people-pleasing tendencies. Through therapy and coaching, she was able to find solutions that helped. This, in her words, basically looked like an outsourcing of everything.

Though Kara was in a better place and had started coaching other physicians in burnout, the pandemic brought a new set of stressors. Her entire practice group needed to shift to telemedicine for their outpatient services, and she spearheaded the system. Telemedicine became something she enjoyed, something she was proud to build. At the same time, the volume of work she was doing for her group and her patients left her treading with her head barely above water. "I was surviving, but I just didn't feel good," she said.

The moment when Kara knew she had to make a drastic change came during one of countless virtual group meetings held outside of work hours. The meeting was about banal subjects, such as how to talk to your patients about smoking, and that's when she realized she couldn't do it anymore. "I needed a new garden," she said.

One of Kara's core values is autonomy. She brainstormed ways that she could incorporate her new love of telemedicine and her passion for coaching in a way that was completely her own. She also saw a need for improved care of patients with eating disorders—another passion of hers, given her ballet background. What she created is a solo telemedicine practice with an emphasis on eating disorder care—something no one else is doing in her geographical area. Her business also includes a coaching arm, for both patients and other physicians.

Kara is now manifesting autonomy, which for her looks like a mixture of telemedicine and coaching between the hours of 9 AM and 2 PM, Monday through Friday. She has complete control over her schedule and her billing (no insurance hassles!). She moved her children to a private school for educational reasons, and she is now active in some of their after-school activities. While her husband has a job that comes with some geographical constraints, he has always wanted to travel more. They're finally making that happen. Most recently, she took a three-month sabbatical that involved both travel and home time.

Through deep introspection during her sabbatical, Kara realized that she needs more quiet, alone time than she's used to giving herself ... more white space, as she likes to call it. "I've never been this happy," she said.

The hardest part about Kara's journey of leaning out has been giving herself permission to do things differently. "There's a lot of tribalism in medicine," she said. She had to let go of beliefs she had about what women should be doing and what doctors should be doing. "I realized there's no right way to do life."

What would Kara tell other women who are contemplating a change like hers? "Look internally for the answers. Have a clear, compelling 'why' to guide you." She also advocates cultivating a nest egg to navigate any financial uncertainty. Revenue from her side gig of physician coaching helped to bridge her startup time and gave her the confidence to keep going.

"It's not that hard," she said. "If you can take care of patients, you are perfectly capable of starting your own business or learning a new technology."

CHAPTER 10
PERMISSION

"Your current safe boundaries were once unknown frontiers."
—unknown

Beyond all the thought traps discussed in Chapter 5, the thing that holds women back most from leaning out is permission. You don't need to wait for external validation from anyone to have permission. You don't need to meet certain criteria or have a specific certification for permission. Also, you don't need to suffer through a major breakdown or life event (like I did) to give yourself permission.

You *have* permission …

… TO TAKE CONTROL OF YOUR HEALTH

Without health, the loftiest of achievements and highest accolades will be meaningless. It just might be necessary to lean out in order to *lean in* to radical self-care. Robin Arzon, one of the most popular instructors for the fitness giant Peloton, used to be a lawyer. As the daughter of immigrants (her mother was a doctor), she was groomed for a high-achieving professional life; health and fitness were not family priorities.

One day during law school, she decided to put on a pair of running shoes to walk to class. Over the next several years she spent as an associate at a New York City law firm, she realized that the times she felt most passionate and most like herself were not when she was at work but when she was exercising. She eventually walked away from law to honor the healthy lifestyle she valued most and become a fitness instructor.

Heather* told me in our initial coaching consultation that she thought she might want to leave her role as director of the pediatrics residency program at her university. She felt drained every day, no matter if she was at home or at the hospital. Her doctor had recently diagnosed her with hypertension and prediabetes. Her relationships with her husband and special needs stepson were suffering.

She felt stuck, overwhelmed, and guilty for not being the badass breadwinner supermom she expected to be 13 years out of residency training. She wanted to figure out her priorities and her career direction, but she wasn't even able to envision how she wanted her days to look.

First we clarified her values. We spent time going through the parts of her workdays that she loves and the parts she loathes. It turned out that harmony was something she greatly valued, and dealing with discipline issues or administrative headaches as program director was a major source of her energy drain. At the same time, she missed doing more clinical work. She loved teaching in action on the hospital floor, but that's not something she was doing much of in her current position. She identified that what she truly desired at work was to hone her clinical skills and leave some of the other stuff behind.

With time, we got to a point where Heather could describe what she wanted to do during a day at home and how to carve out time for personal things such as exercise and meditation (things she had enjoyed in the past). And in between, we busted through a lot of unmet expectations and negative self-talk. We examined her rules and then threw some of them in the garbage.

One of our sessions took place on a day when I was camping in the forest. It was late May, closing in on the end of the academic year. A late spring shower sprinkled on the roof of my RV as I connected to Zoom. Initially, Heather was confused by the change of scenery and asked where I was. The rain beat down harder on the roof. Flustered, she quietly muttered a comment about the director position—the one she had come to me questioning, the one we had been coaching around for months, the one that had been draining her energy for years.

"Well … I guess it's too late now to step down; the new residents are about to come in," she whispered with a smirk. Up until that moment, she had never uttered the phrase, "step down" during our sessions.

Lightning lit the sky, thunder clapped, and it was finally out in the open. "Do you want permission to leave that job? Because you *have* permission. You've had permission all along, and I'm giving you permission again right now," I said. "What do you want to do?"

The next week, Heather made a proposal to her department chief to step down as program director, effective at the end of that academic year, and continue solely as a clinician with some teaching responsibilities. When I last spoke to her, she thanked me for helping her realize she could do it. "I'm exhausted just thinking about being in that old role," she said. "I actually exercised before a work shift the other day! I never would have had the energy to do that before."

... TO IGNORE NAYSAYERS

When you lean out and do something unconventional, you will encounter two types of people: those who are inspired by what you're doing and those who are threatened by it. In my path to lean out, numerous coworkers approached me one on one and told me they'd love to ask for an alternative schedule like I did. Sometimes they shared secret plans to lean out on a time schedule and asked for advice on how to talk to the people in power. As I mentioned earlier, you can be a leader in very quiet ways.

On the other hand, people who are threatened will manifest their feelings in numerous ways. They might profess jealousy but qualify your moves with something like, "Well ... it must be nice to be able to do that because you have _____. I could never do something like that." As a young attending physician, I maximized my time off in academic practice by gaming the vacation system. I wanted to be able to take three- to four-week trips, which is one of the reasons I chose anesthesiology as a specialty. No one else in the department did this. In keeping with my contract, I always made sure I met my minimum number of shifts for the year. In any given month, however, I might not meet the requirement. I played by the rules and never asked for time off during an annual specialty meeting or any other high-request time of year.

I once walked by the physician lounge and overheard coworkers discussing the vacation roster. "She takes a ridiculous amount of vacation! She's way off the charts compared to everyone else. That's not okay," said one exasperated physician, who often compared herself to others. Another shrugged and responded, "She's not in it for the money."

He was right. The old proverb rings true: The person who says it cannot be done should not interrupt the person doing it.

Naysayers might avoid you because your presence reminds them of something they want but can't imagine doing. Naysayers might also be more direct with their disapproval and just flat out tell you that whatever you're doing is not going to work, you're ruining your future career path, etc. Some of these naysayers might be random coworkers. Some might be close friends or family members. You might find that some of your relationships change in ways you hadn't imagined, and that is what's hard.

When faced with naysayers, recall your core values. Remember why you've decided to lean out. Remember that you've earned every right to be where you are in your profession. In today's modern age, pedigrees no longer matter. The only thing that matters is your integrity in your defined scope of work.

In the end, *you* are the most important person in your life; what *you* think takes precedence. It's also helpful to remember that naysayers' attitudes are not a reflection of you but are rather a reflection of how they see themselves. They might feel inadequate, left behind, or angry at themselves for not having the courage to consciously design their lives the way you're designing yours. Their feelings are their responsibility, and you have no need for their approval.

... TO TAKE AN UNEXPECTED DIRECTION

Your vision for work-life balance can look like anything you want it to. Just how you've learned to lean out from the hustle culture, you can lean out from the commonly shared "unconventional" things professionals are doing. Side hustles! Coaching certifications! Short-term rentals! Syndications! If you don't like it or if it's not you, don't do it.

Asha* hired me with a chief complaint of feeling unfulfilled in her current position as a pain management physician. While her interactions with her boss left a lot to be desired, she made excellent money in private practice, worked a reasonable but full-time schedule with a short commute, and had the privilege of performing procedures most days of the week. Many colleagues and friends told her she had "the dream job," but it wasn't *her* dream. She longed for something different; she wanted to perform research. She missed academics, and a position was coming available at a nearby university.

As someone who worked hard to separate myself from the grind and ego of academia, it was difficult to understand on the surface why a professional mom with outside interests who is feeling unfulfilled would want to *add* work (often with roles and expectations that are not particularly well defined) to her plate. When we worked through Asha's core values, it all made sense.

Asha happened to be a first-generation immigrant and the only physician in her family, and one of her greatest values is *leaving a legacy*. She has a husband and children, yes. But if she didn't get a chance to weave her value of legacy into her life, the other things, including her relationships, would likely suffer. We spent the subsequent sessions strategizing her application for an academic pain management position, including a research focus and a special appointment as diversity equity and inclusion leader for the department.

After Asha was accepted and had begun her new position, she told me, "My work transition has gone smoother than expected. It's been reassuring to prove to myself that I can do hard things."

JUST REMEMBER …

You have permission to break your rules, and everyone else's rules, too.

You have permission to take your own path.

You have permission to do what is in your heart, even if it's unexpected.

You don't need to experience a life catastrophe to wake up and do it!

If you take anything from this book, let it be this.

EXERCISE: IDENTIFY YOUR JOY

Think back to a time when you felt truly happy and fulfilled. This could be a moment involving work, or it could be a time when you were immersed in a personal pursuit or spending time with family or friends. It could be a moment when nothing much seemed to be happening. Sometimes those are the best, most joyful moments.

Recall the conditions of your joy. How did it feel in your body? Who was around you? What time of day and year was it? What were you doing during this time? Write it all down and relive it.

KRISTIN'S JOURNEY

"I didn't know how to find that in between, that balance. It took me years to figure that out… I'm still redefining how I define myself."

Kristin* is a family nurse practitioner who spent 12-plus years in the hospital space doing oncology nursing. "I loved taking care of patients, but I didn't love what the work did to me," she said. When she developed some stress-related health problems, it was the wakeup call she needed to decrease her work schedule. "I spent one month taking FMLA and one year upgrading my mindset," she said.

Kristin left a draining managerial role, then gradually transitioned her clinical schedule to two days a week. These moves helped tremendously, and Kristin set out to help other women like her who feel overwhelmed, overworked, and underappreciated. She trained in yoga and integrative health coaching, and she started a small business to offer those services to others.

A few years went by, and Kristin "still felt like my work was holding me back from my kids." She's the mother to three children; two of them are twins, and one has physical and developmental health challenges. Despite crafting a better work-life balance and improving her personal health as a result, "I was still in a spot where I had to pick between family and work."

Kristin craved complete control over her schedule and the ability to do whatever might be needed to help her children. Thus, four years after her initial wake-up call to lean out, Kristin left the bedside without any new work on the horizon. "I knew if I was going to make a big jump, I was going to go all in… It was terrifying," she said.

What helped her most through the time of uncertainty was closely planning every financial move with her husband. Although it was a challenge to their relationship, it was integral for them to face the difficult money conversations. Support from her husband was pivotal, but Kristin says coaching also helped her tremendously in the process.

Kristin now uses her years of experience in cancer care in a consulting role for a research company. She wasn't specifically looking for this type of opportunity but was instead "open to any ways to use my skills where I don't have to sacrifice my wellbeing." Her full-time job is remote and offers complete flexibility.

The hardest part of leaning out for Kristin was playing the long game. "I had to be patient," she said. But the best part has turned out to be a summation of lots of little things. When her daughter gets sick, the world doesn't crumble trying to accommodate everyone's work obligations. She's experiencing peak physical fitness, and she makes all her own food as part of working at home. "And no more Sunday scaries," she added.

Kristin's biggest advice to other women looking to lean out is, "Don't walk the journey alone." She implores women to have the difficult conversations with "whatever a village looks like to you," whether it's a spouse, stakeholders at work, friends, and/or a coach.

CONCLUSION: DESIGN YOUR LIFE

"I hope you find whatever balance you seek with your eyes wide open." —Sheryl Sandberg

This quote was taken from Sandberg's famous Barnard College graduation speech. She then followed it with, "And I hope that you—yes, you—have the ambition to lean in to your career and run the world."

Maybe you do want to run the world. Maybe all you want is to live a life of meaning. Either way, I agree with her: Lifestyle design is something you do with eyes-open intention, apart from the culture that is celebrated by Sandberg's very words.

It's possible that, after reading this book, contemplating the questions, and attempting the exercises, you end up with a work-life balance that looks very similar to a *Lean In* devotee. My client Asha is a great example of someone who, after evaluating her options in light of her core values, chose to transition to a work path that could possibly involve more "work time" than her previous situation. That is perfectly okay—as long as you're consciously choosing it.

It's also possible that you will take that first step off the tread-mill, and it will open even more brain space for reflection. Once my client Rebecca (see Chapter 5) negotiated a decreased schedule with her anesthesiology group, she was able to see other aspects of her work situation that she hadn't noticed before. Her group had been pigeonholing her into doing specific case types due to her subspecialty training, while she wanted a broader practice. She also realized she desired to work in a less cost-driven medical model. Thus, a few months later, Rebecca left her group and began arrange-ments to join an international practice in New Zealand, which also aligned with her family's values of travel, close connec-tion, and adventure.

Rebecca was no longer scared of making a mistake. "I'm making a pivot, and I know now that I can make a different pivot and the world won't fall apart," she said.

THE ASYMPTOTE

Work-life balance is a term that gets a bad rep. This comes from the impossibly perfect imagery of a woman spinning plates in the air with eight arms. The word "achieve" also often comes before the "balance" part. In contradiction, authentic work-life balance is a practice; it's not something that can be achieved. There is no such thing as perfection, and there certainly is no endpoint.

Like the slow, consistent progression of strength that happens when you exercise, balance is not easy, and it's not fast. It's the antithesis of the quick fix. Like my client Heather learned, leaning out can take time. She spent several months doing coaching and introspective work in between to get to the point where my prompt about needing permission jolted her into action. Further, it's possible to stall in your personal discovery and growth from time to time. Life happens, and we must occasionally deviate our focus to tend to family issues, a move, or any other sort of upheaval.

This is perfectly acceptable and part of being a human.

In an interview with Tim Ferris of *Four-Hour Work-week/Body/Chef* fame, Brené Brown, PhD, cautioned, "There is no 'Four-Hour Self-Awareness.'" Law, medicine, and many other professions require continuing education as part of maintaining a license. This makes sense because new innovations and research emerge as time goes on, and there are always things to learn and skills to hone. The term "practice" is therefore fitting. There's always room for improvement and new learning. There is no endpoint where you've become a complete master of your work.

The same is true about mastering your life. Life flows in cycles, and the story of the moment is a Hero's Journey. It starts with the ordinary, the status quo. There is a call to adventure and an initial refusal of the call. Mentors offer advice. A pivotal moment occurs where there's no turning back. There are tests, allies, and enemies. The challenge culminates, and the hero returns with newfound knowledge and transformation. Then it all repeats.

When you take the hero's journey of designing your life, you first depart from the familiar world of *Lean In* culture. You question how you got stuck on the treadmill of achievement and identify what is not working. You venture into the unknown to learn who you are at your core, and you investigate what you really want out of your life and how you want to define success. You come across challenges along the way, and with help from others, you overcome them. You then return to the familiar world, ready to apply your own set of rules to your life, without apology. And at some point in the future, your journey will start again.

CLAIRE'S JOURNEY

"With every step it's okay to be in the moment and think, 'I know what I want. I don't know how this looks long term, but these are the goals and the values that I have.'"

Claire is a physician, mom, creative, and athlete who constantly reinvents her work-life balance. With three babies in tow, she began her professional career in a very busy, production-oriented OB-GYN practice. After working long hours, dedicating herself to developing close patient relationships, and being on call for deliveries every day, she realized her personal values were not in line with those of her group. She lamented the precious time she was losing with her young children. "This was not sustainable for me," she said.

When the CFO told Claire she would likely not make partner because "her numbers" weren't high enough, she asked to cut her work hours. The group did not approve her request, and at the time, laborists/hospitalists were not yet a thing. Given her level of burnout in her specialty, she pivoted to something completely different: a boutique primary care practice with very limited hours. As her children entered high school and college, however, she felt herself again drawn to more robust clinical work in OB-GYN. She spent the hours and money necessary to retrain in the specialty, this time in an international setting. Claire then became one of the only obstetric specialists on the island of Saipan. She later took on more work assignments in Bangladesh, Kenya, Chad, and other countries.

Travel and adventure have always been a part of Claire's value system, and she has now been to every continent and more than 100 countries. The work was "very rewarding, but also very grueling." Witnessing numerous poor birth outcomes due to lack of basic resources like blood and oxygen took an emotional toll on her. In 2018, she took a chance and decided to leave clinical medicine altogether.

In addition to physical and emotional exhaustion, Claire's decision was based on other motivations. She grew up as an only child with parents who were "not hands-on. I kind of raised myself," she said. She knew she wanted to be highly involved with her children, not only during critical times of their development but also when they launched into adulthood. She has helped one of her sons with a business and travels to most of her Nike athlete daughter's running races.

Her current remote job as a hospital administrator gives her the flexibility to travel between coasts to be with her adult children. "I can whittle down [my hours] because I'm a great communicator. I can be anywhere in the world. I can explore. And I can sleep at night," she said. Despite always being an avid exerciser (Claire was a certified yoga instructor and marathon runner), she knew she was missing a huge portion of the key to longevity: sleep. "I realized I want to age well. I want to have peace," she said.

Going from clinical work to hospital administration had some costs. Claire misses the rewarding patient relationships she experienced as an OB-GYN, and she took a substantial pay cut in transition to her nonclinical job. "But I have time wealth," she said. "It's the one commodity you can't make more of. I love being time wealthy."

Aside from exercise and travel, Claire has a passion for videography and drone mapping. Her drone projects sometimes take her to exotic locations, but she's still able to do her hospital administration work remotely. She holds ongoing contracts with universities and the National Park Service as an FAA licensed drone pilot.

Although Claire took the traditional path for a while, she knew she wanted more. She has played the long game of lifestyle design and continues to create a life she loves. Her best advice for other women designing their lives is to spend time finding out what's most important to you. Don't move too quickly, and have a plan that motivates you even if you don't end up sticking to the plan. She also recommends looking to professional Facebook groups and other networks for inspiration, mentoring, and work options you might not have considered.

REVERSIBLE EXPERIMENTS

Designing your life is like cooking. Sometimes you will improvise when resources are limited. Sometimes you will experiment, and that experiment might not go as well as you'd hoped. If that happens, the effect will either be of low significance, or the effect can be reversed to some extent. People are often scared to make changes to their work situations because they think they can't "go back." On the contrary, you often *can* go back—maybe not to the same exact position in the same exact location, but you'll likely be able to recreate whatever it is you're missing.

Cheri (see Chapter 8) has conducted many such experiments, and she has been surprised every time at what she's learned.

Changes to her work-life balance that seemed like no-brainers were not always as great as she expected. In contrast, changes she wasn't so sure about sometimes surprised her. "I was wrong about myself so many times," she said.

You must experiment to find out; you must risk, and sometimes experience, failure. Jen Sincero said, "The only failure is quitting. Everything else is just gathering information."

A few years ago, a colleague left her position in academic medicine to move to a different state. The family members who had served as her trusted childcare needed to move, so she moved with them. On top of her clinical and research duties, she served as the head of a subspecialty teaching group, and as a single mother to two children, she needed reliable help at home. At the same time, the weight of these work roles was causing tremendous stress. She would lash out at the trainees, and she frankly was not the friendliest person to work with.

A year went by in her new position with a private practice group out of state and the same family babysitters. Despite having her trusty childcare team, she just wasn't happy in her new situation. She missed the academic environment and her old hometown. She negotiated to return to the department, but her previous role as group leader was not available anymore. She found a new nanny, but it turned out that she needed less flexibility in her childcare now that her job was a little different … simpler. This "return with a twist" brought back the calm, collected coworker people had remembered from years before.

The amazing thing about the human penchant for the hedonic treadmill is that it works both ways. Our happiness returns to baseline even after we achieve more money, possessions, awards, etc. Alternatively, when bad things happen—like failures, setbacks, or even loss—our happiness levels also return to steady state over time. Allow yourself to experiment and know that you might make some mistakes. It will be okay.

YOU ARE IN CONTROL

Our professional paths are filled with complexities often beyond our control—patient load, mandatory meetings or trainings, client needs, the operating room schedule, the madness of tax season. Simultaneously, we are immersed in a culture that deters us from being our authentic selves at work. Assuming the mantle of changing external factors or culture is not an easy task, but there is something you can do right now.

You can lean out from hustling to feel worthy. You can lean out from subscribing to inauthentic metrics of success. You can lean out from living to meet others' expectations. In turn, you can lean in to your authentic voice as it tells you what you really want your life to look like.

One thing is certain: *You* are in control of how you design your work and life. With the tools presented in this book, you have the ability to activate your self-awareness and clearly envision what you want. Your new self-knowledge will give you the confidence to take the steps, place the boundaries, and ask for what you want. And if your asks and boundaries are not met, you will explore alternatives with curiosity.

Balance does exist, and you deserve to have it. What does it look like for you?

On a late fall afternoon, I peer over the edge of the bank at the stream bed below. The yellowed grass is darkening as the sun begins to hide behind the pink cliffs above the surrounding valley. I'm holding hands with the child I struggled for years to bring into this world, the child I so desperately wanted more than any degree, certification, or accolade. She is the child who inspired me to gradually lean out more and more at work so I could know her fully. She's the reason we're standing here after making this shift to a rural, off-grid existence.

The sound of the water flowing in the stream reminds me of music. There are other sounds, too—chirping birds, snapping grasshoppers, and the distinctive quaking of aspen leaves. It's like a miniature orchestral ensemble performing just for us.

Yesterday, I treated patients at a nearby surgery center so a colleague could take a vacation. Tomorrow, I'll meet with a coaching client and film an inspirational yoga practice in the meadow to share with other professionals in need of some moments of mindfulness and flow. Tonight, I'll read a bedtime story to my child before working on a wellness talk for an upcoming medical conference. Today, I did a little homeschooling, a little playing, and some hiking—and a whole lot of loving in this quiet and beautiful place.

This is my balance.

If you enjoyed this book and would like to read more about the topics presented herein, please consider signing up as a subscriber to my blog, newsletter, and the new Lean Out podcast at www.PracticeBalance.com. If you found this book helpful, please leave a review on Amazon, share your thoughts on social media, and consider gifting this book to another woman who needs to hear this information.
Thank you!

RESOURCES

GENERAL

www.practicebalance.com: The Practice Balance blog, newsletter, and Lean Out podcast

INFERTILITY

Websites for information and guidance when navigating a fertility journey:

- Resolve: https://www.resolve.org
- SART: https://www.sart.org
- ASRM: https://www.asrm.org

Facebook support groups: These have been tremendously helpful for navigating infertility and other work-life balance issues. However, some of them are not searchable. The name of the one searchable infertility group for physicians is Women Physician Infertility Group (IVF/IUI). I'm sure these exist for other professions as well; do a little research and reach out to women in your Facebook network to find them.

Also, you can find a variety of active groups for the general population by going to the Groups tab and searching a keyword such as "infertility." For example, typing this word into the search bar brings up several groups with various focuses, containing anywhere from 300 to 81,000 members. Enjoy the support, but always take the advice with a grain of salt.

SELF-KNOWLEDGE

Assessments:

- Quiet Introvert vs. Extrovert: https://susancain.net/ quiet-quiz
- Four Tendencies: https://gretchenrubin.com/quiz
- Five Love Languages: https://5lovelanguages.com/ quizzes/love-language
- MBTI: https://eu.themyersbriggs.com/en/ tools/MBTI
- Enneagram: https://tests.enneagraminstitute.com
- CliftonStrengths: https://www.gallup.com/ cliftonstrengths/en/253868/popular-cliftonstrengths-assessment-products.aspx

EXCELLENT BOOKS

On happiness:

- Arthur Brooks, *From Strength to Strength: Finding Success, Happiness, and Deep Purpose in the Second Half of Life*
- Mo Gawdat, *Solve for Happy: Engineer Your Path to Joy*

On self compassion:

- Kristin Neff, *Fierce Self-Compassion: How Women Can Harness Kindness to Speak Up, Claim Their Power and Thrive*
- Kristin Neff and Christopher Germer, *The Mindful Self-Compassion Workbook: A Proven Way to Accept Yourself, Build Inner Strength, and Thrive*

On boundaries:

- Sasha Shillcutt, *Brave Boundaries: Strategies to Say No, Stand Strong, and Take Control of Your Time*
- Greg McKeown, *Essentialism: The Disciplined Pursuit of Less*

On financial freedom:

- JL Collins, *The Simple Path to Wealth: Your Road Map to Financial Independence and a Rich, Free Life*
- Vicki Robin, *Your Money or Your Life: 9 Steps to Transforming Your Relationship with Money and Achieving Financial Independence*

COACHING

- Practice Balance Coaching (my coaching services): https://www.practicebalance.com
- Physician Coaching Alliance: https://www.physiciancoachingalliance.com

FINANCIAL FREEDOM

- Choose FI: https://www.choosefi.com

- White Coat Investor: https://www.whitecoatinvestor.com
- Physician on FIRE: https://www.physicianonfire.com

LIST OF SKILLS

Accounting	Engineering	Modeling	Professionalism
Active Listening	Explaining	Negotiation	Reliability
Adaptability	Flexibility	Networking	Research
Coaching	Forecasting	Organization	Service
Collaboration	Giving Feedback	Operations	Social Media
Computing	Graphic Design	Optimization	Supervising
Communication	Informatics	Problem Solving	SEO
Creativity	Interpretation	Product Development	Systems
Customer Service	Law	Project Management	Teaching
Data Analysis	Leadership	Programming	Translation
Design	Mathematics	Public Speaking	Videography
Development	Management	Procedures	Websites
Diagnosis	Marketing	Photography	Writing
Documentation	Medicine	Quality Control	
Editing	Mentoring	Quality Improvement	

LIST OF STRENGTHS

Achiever	Enthusiastic	Logical	Relationship Builder
Action	Fair	Mindful	Responsible
Adventurous	Flexible	Moderate	Strategic
Analytical	Focused	Motivating	Self-aware
Authentic	Friendly	Mystical	Spiritual
Caring	Futuristic	Nurturing	Successful
Communicator	Generous	Organizer	Team-oriented
Compassionate	Grateful	Optimistic	Thoughtful
Connected	Helpful	Optimizer	Trustworthy
Considerate	Honest	Patient	Versatile
Creative	Idealistic	Persuasive	Visionary
Dedicated	Independent	Persistent	Welcoming
Disciplined	Inspirational	Positive	Wise
Dreamer	Kind	Practical	
Empath	Learner	Relator	

LIST OF VALUES

Accomplishment	Determination	Initiative	Personal growth
Acceptance	Discipline	Innovation	Pleasure
Achievement	Discovery	Integrity	Power
Adventure	Diversity	Inner peace	Privacy
Assertiveness	Education	Intensity	Problem solving
Authenticity	Efficiency	Intimacy	Professionalism
Autonomy	Environment	Intuition	Prosperity
Balance	Equality	Joy	Progress
Beauty	Excellence	Justice	Respect
Caring	Excitement	Kindness	Romance
Challenge	Fairness	Knowledge	Safety
Change	Faith	Leadership	Security
Clarity	Family	Learning	Self-control
Commitment	Fitness	Love	Self-development
Communication	Flexibility	Loyalty	Skillfulness
Community	Freedom	Meaning	Spirituality
Compassion	Friendship	Merit	Strength
Competence	Frugality	Mindfulness	Straightforwardness
Competition	Fulfillment	Moderation	Success
Confidence	Fun	Modesty	Teamwork
Conformity	Generosity	Money	Timeliness
Connection	Genuineness	Nature	Tradition
Conservation	Goodness	Nurturing	Tranquility
Contribution	Gratitude	Openness	
Cooperation	Harmony	Optimism	Trust
Courage	Healing	Open-mindedness	Truth
Curiosity	Health	Order	Unity
Creativity	Honesty	Patience	Variety
Credibility	Humility	Patriotism	Vitality
Decisiveness	Improvement	Peace	Wealth
Dedication	Independence	Perseverance	Wisdom
Democracy	Individuality	Persistence	

REFERENCES

CHAPTER 2

1. Belkin, D. A Generation of Men Give Up on College: 'I Just Feel Lost'. *Wall Street Journal*, Sept 6, 2021.
2. https://www.nytimes.com/2016/12/16/business/dealbook/women-majority-of-us-law-students-first-time.html
3. Boyle, P. More Women Than Men Are Enrolled in Medical School. *AAMC News* www.aamc.org, Dec 19, 2019.
4. https://www.weforum.org/agenda/2022/03/ceos-fortune-500-companies-female
5. Sandberg, S. *Lean In: Women, Work, and the Will to Lead*. Knopf, 1st edition, 2013.
6. https://www.cdc.gov/diabetes/data/statistics-report/index.html
7. https://www.cdc.gov/nchs/data/nhanes/databriefs/adultweight.pdf
8. https://www.heart.org/en/about-us/heart-and-stroke-association-statistics
9. Descatha, A *et al*. The Effect of Exposure to Long Hours on Stroke: A Systematic Review and Meta Analysis From the WHO/ILO Joint Estimates of the Work-Related Burden of Disease and Injury. https://doi.org/10.1016/j.envint.2020.105746
10. https://www2.deloitte.com/us/en/pages/about-deloitte/articles/burnout-survey.html
11. Palmer, J and L Ouyang. Analysis: Survey Finds Lawyer Burnout Rising, Well-Being Falling. *Bloomberg Law*, Jun 28, 2021.
12. Kane, L. Medscape National Physician Burnout and Suicide Report 2020: The Generational Divide. https://www.medscape.com/slideshow/2020-lifestyle-burnout-6012460?faf=1
13. Four Surveys Find Female Physicians Experience More Burnout. *Becker's Hospital Review*, Sep 14, 2022.

CHAPTER 3

1. Key Statistics from the National Survey of Family Growth-- Infertility and Impaired Fecundity. Centers for Disease Control National Center for Health Statistics. https://www.cdc.gov/nchs/nsfg/key_statistics/i-keystat.htm#infertility.

2. Stentz, NV *et al*. Fertility and childbearing among American female physicians. *J Womens Health* (Larchmt). 2016;25:1059-1065.

3. Ouzzzani S and N Southerland. Why Lawyers Need to Talk About Infertility. ALM/law.com, Jan 2002.

4. Reproductive Facts from the American Society of Reproductive Medicine. https://www.reproductivefacts.org/faqs/quick-facts-about-infertility/

5. A Medical Career at a Cost: Infertility. https://www.nytimes.com/2021/09/13/health/women-doctors-infertility.html

6. Source Document: The Impact of Age on Female. American Society of Reproductive Medicine. https://www.sart.org/globalassets/asrm/asrm-content/learning--resources/patient-resources/protect-your-fertility3/age_femaleinfertility.pdf

7. Rangel EL et al. Incidence of infertility and pregnancy complications in US female surgeons. *JAMA Surg*. 2021 Oct 1;156(10):905-915.

8. Domar, A. The relationship between stress and infertility. *Fertility and Sterility*, Mar 29, 2020. https://www.fertstertdialog.com/posts/64455-domar-consider-this?room_id=101-consider-this

9. Baker, D. The Hidden Costs of Physician Infertility. https://opmed.doximity.com/articles/the-hidden-costs-of-physician-infertility

CHAPTER 4

1. Etherson, ME. Portraying a False Self: Perfectionism and Inauthenticity. *Psychology Today*, Jan 30, 2020.

2. https://www.psychologytoday.com/intl/basics/hedonic-treadmill

CHAPTER 5

1. What You Don't Learn in Medical School with Julie Foucher. The Dr. Gabrielle Lyon Podcast #6.
2. Weinberg, YJ *et al.* Gender Differences in Personality Across the Ten Aspects of the Big Five. *Front Psychol._* 2011; 2: 178.
3. Dweck, C. *Mindset: The New Psychology of Success.* Ballatine Books, Updated edition, 2007.
4. Puderbaugh, M and PD Emmady. Neuroplasticity. *Stat Pearls*, May 8, 2022.
5. Porter, J *et al.* Revisiting the Time Needed to Provide Adult Primary Care. *J Gen Int Med* Jul 2022.
6. Lawyer Burnout: How Toxic Workplaces Create Burned Out Attorneys. JD Nation Blog, Feb 3 2022.
7. https://www.chasejarvis.com/blog/old-rules-no-longer-apply/
8. Bruk, A *et al.* (2018). Beautiful mess effect: Self–other differences in evaluation of showing vulnerability. *Journal of Personality and Social Psychology,* 115(2), 192–205.
9. Brown, B. *Atlas of the Heart: Mapping Meaningful Connection and the Language of Human Experience.* Random House, First Edition, 2021.

CHAPTER 6

1. https://www.chasejarvis.com/blog/jason-reynolds-freedom-to-breathe-finding-self-when-no-one-is-looking/
2. Tolle, E. *A New Earth: Awakening to Your Life's Purpose*. Penguin, 2008. p 214.
3. Baker, D. The Hidden Costs of Physician Infertility. Doximity Op-Med, April 18, 2022. https://www.doximity.com/articles/748110d4-911d-4232-8e8c-b14c6c32330b
4. Bruk, A *et al.* (2018). Beautiful mess effect: Self–other differences in evaluation of showing vulnerability. *Journal of Personality and Social Psychology,* 115(2), 192–205.
5. www.positiveintelligence.com

CHAPTER 7

1. Neff, K and C Germer. *The Mindful Self-Compassion Workbook: A Proven Way to Accept Yourself, Build Inner Strength, and Thrive.* The Guilford Press, 2018.
2. https://susancain.net/quiet-quiz/#
3. https://gretchenrubin.com/quiz/
4. https://5lovelanguages.com/quizzes

CHAPTER 8

1. The Science of Happiness with Arthur Brooks. The Peter Attia Drive Podcast #226, 10/10/2022.

CHAPTER 9

1. David, Susan. *Emotional Agility: Get Unstuck, Embrace Change, and Thrive in Work and Life.* Avery, 2016.
2. Bonus: Sleep When You're Dead Tired (LIVE with Arianna Huffington). The Happiness Lab Podcast, 1/26/2020.
3. Rudd, M et al (2012). Awe Expands People's Perception of Time, Alters Decision Making, and Enhances Wellbeing. *Psychological Science* 23(10): 1130-1136.
4. Dusek, Heidi. Beyond Normal: A Field Guide to Embrace Adventure, Explore the Wilderness, and Design an Extraordinary Life With Kids. Harshman House Publishing, 2022.
5. 4-7-8 Breathing: Health Benefits and Demonstration. https://www.drweil.com/videos-features/videos/the-4-7-8-breath-health-benefits-demonstration/
6. https://www.positiveintelligence.com/science
7. McKeown, G. *Essentialism: The Disciplined Pursuit of Less.* Virgin Books, 2014.

8. Dyrbye, LN *et al.* Effects of a Professional Coaching Intervention on the Wellbeing and Distress of Physicians: A Pilot Randomized Clinical Trial. *JAMA Intern Med.* 2019;179(10):1406-1414.

9. Collins, JL. *The Simple Path to Wealth: Your Roadmap to Financial Independence and a Rich, Free Life*. CreateSpace Independence Publishing, 2016.

ACKNOWLEDGMENTS

Thank you, dear readers of this book, my blog, and my social media musings, for your continued support. Thanks also to my past coaching clients for the privilege of helping you on your journeys to leaning out.

Thanks to the women physician members of multiple Facebook groups, notably Stay At Home MD, Bad Mom Docs, Women Physician Entrepreneurs, Women Physician Writers, Doctors on Social Media, and Physician Anesthesiologist Mom Group, for the continued support, inspiration, CME, and "beta."

I appreciate those who've given me a platform to grow and spread my messages via their blogs, podcasts, or conferences. These include Jim Dahle (The White Coat Investor), Kevin Pho (KevinMD), Sasha Shillcutt (Brave Enough), the ladies of Physician Coaching Alliance, Bonnie Koo (Wealthy Mom MD), Brent Lacey (The Scope of Practice), Leif Dahleen (Physician on FIRE), and others.

Without inspiring stories from the numerous women professionals profiled in this book, it wouldn't be what it is. Thank you, ladies, for sharing your journeys with me and the world.

I'm also grateful to the numerous women who provided feedback on the content in this book.

Thanks to my editor and publisher Jennifer Bright for her support and advice during the book writing process. In addition, I'd like to thank my colleague, beta reader, muse, editor, and friend BC Krygowski for all her suggestions and unwavering encouragement.

This book is written for every woman who aspires to achieve with balance, but especially for my daughter, Aspen, to whom this book is dedicated. Thank you for being patient with me as I created these words. May you not need 40-plus years to understand them and instead begin designing your authentic balance from the start.

Lastly, I'd like to thank my husband, Trent Baker, for always serving as a built-in coach and role model for how to design your life. You've been this and so many other things to me for the past 30 years. I'm so happy we've taken this path together.

ABOUT THE AUTHOR

Dawn L. Baker, MD, MS, is a physician, wife, mother, and minimalist entrepreneur. She spent the early years of her adult life traveling the world to rock climb. This experience informed the way she approached her professional career, where she's bucked the traditional picture of what a doctor looks like and instead designed her own authentic work-life balance.

Dawn earned her BS and MS degrees in chemical engineering at the University of Arizona, between which she worked at both a small tech startup and a large semiconductor corporation. After spending a year traveling and living at various climbing destinations all over the world, she realized she desired a career path that involved service and broader human connections. She later completed medical school and subspecialty training at the University of Utah. Dawn became a board-certified anesthesiologist in 2013 and continues to practice medicine on a part-time basis.

A cancer and infertility survivor, Dawn started the website practicebalance.com to help other physicians and professionals improve their overall wellness and balance. Her work has been featured by the White Coat Investor, Brave Enough, Physician on FIRE, and Mothers in Medicine, in addition to national syndicates such as KevinMD and Doximity.

Dawn's adventures have evolved from steep rock walls to hiking trails and playgrounds since the birth of her daughter in 2015. She is a published author, keynote speaker, certified yoga instructor (RYT200), and life coach. In 2021, she and her husband purchased a large piece of property on the high plateaus of southern Utah, where they have been living and building an off-grid homestead. Dawn remains a perpetual lover of fitness, personal development, and nature walks with her family.

Printed in the USA
CPSIA information can be obtained
at www.ICGtesting.com
JSHW010506271223
54282JS00008B/24